Distribution and Differentiation of Youth

A Study of Transition from
School to College

Distribution and Differentiation of Youth

A Study of Transition From School to College

Dale Tillery

Center for Research
and Development in
Higher Education

University of California, Berkeley

Ballinger Publishing Company ● Cambridge, Mass.
A Subsidiary of J.B. Lippincott Company

Library of Congress Catalog Card Number: 73-9578

International Standard Book Number: 0-88410-152-5

Printed in the United States of America

Library of Congress Cataloging in Publication Data

Tillery, Dale.

Distribution and differentiation of youth.

Bibliography: p.
1. High school seniors. 2. Student aspirations. 3. High school students' socio-economic status. 4. College attendance. I. Title.
LB2350.T54   373.1'8   73-9578
ISBN 0-88410-152-5

Table of Contents

Figures

Tables

Acknowledgments

A number of individuals and groups have contributed to the SCOPE Project generally and to this publication specifically. The funding agencies—the College Entrance Examination Board and the Center for Research and Development in Higher Education of the University of California—have made this study possible.

Sam Kendrick and, before him, Warren Willingham have been particularly helpful to the SCOPE staff during the project years of 1965 to 1972. These two men, along with Don Karl and his colleagues in the publication division of CEEB, have helped in many ways and have earned our gratitude.

To Denis Donovan, Barbara Sherman, and Rudy Melone, who served on the SCOPE staff, go our thanks for substantive contributions to this report. The efficient processing of great amounts of data resulted from the planning and talents of Charles Gehrke, George Myland, and Diana Fackenthal. In the closing months of our work we have had the splendid contributions of Claire Alameda and Sarah Walker, project secretaries; Jerry Ball and Jeff Weissman, special assistants; and Ted Kildegaard and Carol Omelich who are working on other publications.

No one has been more helpful in the preparation of this manuscript than Charles Collins, Dean of Los Medanos College. During the summer of 1972 he worked with me and my staff in revising the initial manuscript. This book reflects his thoughtful understanding of the issues of who goes to college, where, and what for. Like myself, he shares a certain pride in the increasing participation of youth in postsecondary education, but is profoundly disturbed by the separation of youth by the system into educational "haves" and "have nots."

In thanking these people who have worked directly with us, we are also mindful of the contributions made by students, the subjects of our study, and their teachers, counselors, school administrators, and the officials of the wide array of colleges attended by the SCOPE students.

Distribution and Differentiation of Youth

A Study of Transition from School to College

Chapter One

Questions to Pose and Answers to Seek

This study concerns itself with what happens educationally at the juncture between late childhood and youth. In direct contrast to previous times and other societies, the possible branchings into distinct life options are many. A youth today has a large number of choices facing him, and few of these choices are direct and simple. A high school senior now must not only choose whether or not to attend college but also decide what the various reasons are for choosing. When a ghetto-born, black female of seventeen chooses college over marriage, work, or oblivion, even the mode of choosing may differ from that of a Caucasian, middle-class male of the same age. It is this diversity that is so puzzling for researchers and consumers alike who seek to interpret data from studies of students. Consider that in America in the industrial age, even the grandparents of today's youth had relatively few choices, and most of these were predetermined. Only 4 percent went to college; indeed, only 6 percent of the appropriate age group graduated from high school, and, needless to say, most of those in the college stream were middle- to upper-class white males [U.S. Department of Commerce 1970].

But what about this complex, pluralistic society in the third quarter of the twentieth century? What happened, for example, to the class of 1966? What kind of culling and channeling took place among the 1966 high school seniors in a Northeastern, a Southern, a Midwestern, and a Western state that routed some youth to universities, some to four-year colleges, some to junior colleges, some to special schools, and some to a world of which college was not a part? What are the useful questions to be asked and where does the significance of the answers lie?

LOOKING FOR THE ANSWERS

Obviously, options have to exist before choices can be made. If (contrary to fact) one of the sample states had only private universities and very few of these, then the youth of that state would have one of three options: qualify as one of the select few, forget about college, or go to another state where there were more options. And, of course, states do differ in the educational options open to youth. Accessibility to college does become a determinant of how many go to college and who they will be. The number and type of colleges in California, Illinois, Massachusetts, and North Carolina will be reported in this study and implications drawn of who goes where.

One gross fact that is already known is that high school graduation marks a crucial branching, with some youth moving into the college world and other young people channeled into the noncollege world. The distinction between *youth* and *young people* is made advisedly because college extends the period characterized by all those qualities connoted in the term youth whereas those entering the noncollege world leave youth, to a large degree, behind them. Because it is a crossroad, it is important to know the factors that appear to determine the choices. Research provides parsimonious explanations based on ability, social class, sex, race, and other determinants, but measure needs to be taken of even these obvious influences, and perhaps in the process more subtle determinants will also be found.

Up through high school young people have, perhaps at route step, marched along together. At about eighteen years of age, whatever loose formation they had breaks up, and more than half of them continue in the directions marked *higher education* even though they take roads of varying lengths and difficulty, leading to varying rewards. In the longitudinal SCOPE Project,[1] of which this report is a part, the group who veered off from higher education will be kept in mind, even though they are now a minority. The focus here, however, will be on the slightly larger group who, by chance or design, continued on to post secondary education.

There are several categorical measures that need to be taken. Are those youth in the college stream mostly men, as was once the case? Obviously not, yet there is differential channeling by sex. How this occurs will be discussed later. Are there different tracks to private as opposed to public colleges and universities? Obviously yes, but the answer is much more complex than that and will be analyzed in this study. A third categorical measure is that of race. In the past, the college group would have been notably whiter, with a small, separate black stream and, as Malcolm X once put it, "a few flies in the buttermilk." The high school seniors in 1966 were only in the first grade when

---

1. SCOPE is a longitudinal study of student decision-making during the secondary school years of large samples of students in California, Illinois, Massachusetts, and North Carolina. The project funded by the College Entrance Examinations Board, focussed on 2 chart groups; seniors of 1966 who were then followed to postsecondary institutions the following year, and groups of 9th graders who were studied annually, including their entrance to college in 1970.

the Supreme Court ruled in 1954 that by definition separate schools were un-
equal schools and were, therefore, in violation of the equal protection clause
of the United States Constitution. There were a dozen years to make the faces
of the college students as multicolored as Joseph's coat, to achieve a racial balance in educational opportunity. Some beginning evidence of this balance is in
and will be reported. A much more difficult issue to address is whether race
can be viewed as a separate determinant or as part of a syndrome.

There is a wealth of psychological evidence suggesting that people
do what they are expected to do or, put a different way, their self-concept
grows largely from the acted-out perceptions that "significant others" have of
them. To the extent this is true, student attitudes about going to college will
follow from parent attitudes about going to college. Consequently, student
attitudes about college and student perceptions of parent attitudes about
college were compared and analyzed.

The words *free higher education* are heard often and have a nice
ring to them. Rhetoric aside, the fact is that going to college costs money. In
some cases it may not mean much out-of-pocket money, but even then, it does
mean that no money, or less money, is coming into the pocket and home. This
financial determinant is hard to separate from that of socioeconomic class.
Even so, it needs to be separated, for many aspects of student financing of higher education are independent of parents' affluence or poverty.

In most life issues, early and definite decision is a rough index of
the amount of commitment to a course of action. Decisions about going to college are major life issues and, presumably, those youth who have made clear and
early decisions not only have built up psychological commitments but have also
taken the preparatory steps that make acting out the decision inevitable and
probably easier. Of course, the finding that early deciders are more likely to
attend college is not worth much. Answers still have to be sought to the question
of what factors make for early decision. Better understanding of these factors
then leads to speculation on whether the effort of counseling to secure an early
decision, even when factors normally related to early decision are absent, would
result in development of commitment and the acting out (enrollment in college)
of this commitment.

It was just suggested that counseling itself might become an inter-
vening variable, a determinant in whether or not high school graduates opt for
college. Certainly, young people are influenced in their decision-making. The
question is, by whom? On the face of it, professional counsel would seem more
valuable than amateur counsel; advice from trained counselors would seem
worth more than peer counseling. More often than not, parents are also ama-
teurs in vocational and educational guidance. And even teachers may or may not
dispense accurate information about careers and the best way to prepare for
them. But this is argument by common sense, not by data. The findings report-

ed here will be concerned with who the students perceived as being influential participants in their decision-making processes.

All of the determinants introduced thus far relate most directly to that first either-or question: whether to join the college world or the world of work (or unemployment). Assuming that this first big decision is for the college stream, the determinants also become factors in selecting the channel within the stream. This is even more true of those traditional determinants of academic aptitude, academic achievement, and socioeconomic status. The point is that in some states aptitude, grades, and social class, no matter how low, would not necessarily bar the student at the first branching. He might stay in the college stream, but which channel he would follow within that stream would be highly dependent upon each of these traditional factors. Data on these variables is in copious supply and will be used in different ways to show, perhaps for the first time, how the differential channeling of high school graduates to college takes place.

The broad category labeled "senior colleges" is confusing in its imprecision. It has value when the aim is to distinguish between categories such as the four-year college vis-à-vis the junior college. But, for example, Harvard and the University of California are as different from a small, church-related, four-year college as that college is from a junior college. A more refined analysis of selection is needed, and such an analysis has been made. The attraction or pull that different kinds of institutions, particularly Ph.D.-granting universities, have on varying groups of students will be reported.

Each of these and other determinants in the process of deciding whether to attend and then choosing a college will be brought into separate focus, one by one, and some conclusions and implications unique to that variable will be drawn. Needless to say, the determinants are not mutually exclusive. They meld and interact so that the whole is different from the simple addition of all the parts. Therefore, the concluding chapter in this report will, with more freedom to speculate, try to bring a broader meaning to all the data presented and its many implications. This, in turn, will anticipate the later reporting of biographical and multivariate studies on SCOPE students who were closely followed from grade nine in 1966 to entry into college in 1969. But before reporting the substance of the present research, it is necessary first to describe how the study was done.

Chapter Two

The Scope Project

Two groups of high school students cooperated with the SCOPE Project:
33,965 seniors in the sping of 1966 from California, Illinois, Massachusetts,
and North Carolina and 46,118 ninth grade students from the same states and
school districts. The twelfth graders, who are the subjects of this report, were
followed into postsecondary life to determine if and where they went to
college. In turn, the grade nine students were studied annually as they moved
through secondary school, and then those who went to college in 1969-70
were again studied near the close of the freshman year. The resulting longitudinal data on these two groups of subjects represents a major source of information about certain behavior, attitudes, educational decisions, and outcome of
young people in different regions of the United States. The SCOPE staff as
well as researchers across the country are using this data bank to answer diverse questions about students, particularly about their perceptions and
experiences in school and college.

THE PRIMARY STUDIES

Whereas this report will focus on the distribution of various groups of 1966
seniors across different types of postsecondary institutions, the longitudinal
studies of the ninth grade students of 1966 will give primary attention to
the processes and outcomes of decision-making during the school years. This,
the 1966 senior component of the project can be viewed as the pilot study for
a five-year follow-up of the contemporary ninth graders only in the sense that
it provided a testing ground for the pursuit of college-goers and for testing relationships between characteristics of high school students with specific postsecondary outcomes. In brief, this is a descriptive study of who went to college
and where. It offers multiple but partial explanations for diverse outcomes of
the seniors from the project states. The five-year longitudinal study, on the

other hand, seeks by multivariate and biographical techniques to put the pieces together from home, school, and peer relationships in order to understand, over time, the dynamics and behavior of educational choice.

SPONSORSHIP AND PURPOSES

School to College: Opportunities for Postsecondary Education (SCOPE) is a longitudinal study of students sponsored by the Center for Research and Development in Higher Education (CRDHE) and by the College Entrance Examination Board (CEEB). CEEB has been the primary source of financial support for SCOPE and has also provided technical assistance through its regional and New York offices, its educational advisory committees, and its publication division. The CRDHE at the University of California has directed and conducted the project as part of its continuing research-and-development focus on students in higher education. Together, these sponsoring organizations conceived SCOPE as a means of "discovering the decision-making patterns among high school students—the ways in which they acquire information about colleges and vocations; the nature and relative importance of parental, school, and general community influences on their decisions; and when various stages in the decision-making process occur" [Tillery, Donovan, and Sherman 1966b, p.1]. The project, at a time when great demands were being made on American schools, received the active and sustained cooperation of teachers and administrators in schools, colleges, and educational systems. No one, of course, contributed more than the students who are the subjects of this and other reports. Although the project, as such, terminated in the fall of 1971, a SCOPE Information Center is being maintained in Berkeley so that the staffs of the CRDHE and CEEB as well as other researchers can continue to use the massive data base for continuing research.

THE 1966 GRADE TWELVE SAMPLES

In order to have sufficient subjects from groups of students with different characteristics and with diverse outcomes for the analyses being reported, the following samples of grade twelve students were selected from the four states:

California	7,567
Illinois	8,600
Massachusetts	6,335
North Carolina	11,377

Among other things, the differences in sample sizes reflected anticipated differences in the incidence of college attendance in 1966. This ideal was slightly biased by the failure of less than 10 percent of the seniors across the states to participate through absenteeism or personal preference:

> A more serious source of bias may be the loss of a metropolitan school district in each of three states—California, Illinois, and Massachusetts. Although the three districts chose not to participate, adjacent alternative schools in California and Illinois volunteered and became part of the SCOPE Project. It would appear that proper representation of these two areas has thus been reestablished. [Ibid., p. 4].

In Massachusetts the large metropolitan area that failed to participate could not be replaced; therefore, that state's public school enrollments are underrepresented. Its nonpublic shcools, however, are well represented throughout the state. In spite of these losses, the size of the samples and the range of types of participating schools means that data accurately reflects the attitudes, abilities, and interests of a remarkable cross section of youth in the public and private schools of the SCOPE states. Specifically, the number of schools that participated in the SCOPE Project were: California, 32 public and 12 nonpublic; Illinois, 46 public and 18 nonpublic; Massachusetts, 28 public and 21 nonpublic; and North Carolina, 138 public and 4 nonpublic. In the follow-up of the 1966 seniors, approximately 1,500 colleges and other post-secondary schools cooperated.

SOURCES AND AREAS OF DATA

Data was collected by sets of tests and questionnaires administered in two sessions by staff members of the participating schools. Among the data collected at this time were specific college preferences and other locator information which were used in the intense follow-up of college-goers one year later. Validation of college enrollment was provided by registrars from the post-secondary institutions of the nation. Again, the schools and the public two-year colleges were particularly helpful in locating students who did not matriculate to any of the colleges they said they preferred while in high school.

Academic Ability

With concern for economy of time in collecting initial data about students, care was taken to select measures of academic abilities that would correlate highly with standard instruments used in American schools and that could be administered with maximum ease within a standard class period. The Academic Ability Test (AAT), which had been developed by Educational Testing Service, seemed appropriate for this task. The AAT correlated very highly with the School and College Ability Test; it was easy to administer within a fifty-minute period; and it gave verbal, mathematical, and total scores.

To be sure, the SCOPE staff shared the concerns of practicing educators and researchers in the field of educational testing regarding the appropriateness of many standard tests in measuring the abilities of educationally handicapped youngsters. It was not assumed, therefore, that the distributions of scores from these instruments described with accuracy the abilities of all youngsters tested. In particular, students with reading problems and deficits in other areas of educational experience are handicapped on these as well as related ability tests. Nevertheless, both students and school personnel, in practice, use such test scores in measuring achievement during the school years and predicting success in higher education. In reference to these measures, group characteristics are highly important and were used in studying educational and career choices.

The large and generally representative nature of the state samples provides quite helpful normative information about these tests and their distributions, means, and standard deviations.

Family and Home Milieu

A considerable number of inquiries tapping different aspects of home and family life have been included in this research. Three major considerations led to the selection of these variables. The first and most basic concern was for the influence of the family, not only in affecting the present choice behavior of students but also for understanding the antecedents of this behavior. Parents have the earliest and probably the most pervasive influence on the decisions that students make about school and career. It is essential to know both about the general characteristics of the home and about the student's perceptions of his relation to others in this milieu.

The second consideration concerns the development of meaningful and stable sets of indices of socioeconomic status with which to classify students in analyzing what they think and do about educational and career choices. Given the diversity of information about home backgrounds, SCOPE empirically explored the varied dimensions of socioeconomic status and identified the particular variables that help best to define common patterns of decision-making.

The third factor concerns the need to understand differences in the post-high school plans of students of *similar* socioeconomic status. Previous research suggests that a father's occupation is one of the most reliable measures in distinguishing between students who go to college and those who don't go. Yet this gross distinction sheds little light on the differences that exist within the college group or within the noncollege group.

To approach questions of this nature, it is necessary to consider the more subtle ways in which parents' and home influence decision-making. For example, father's occupation as such may be of less significance than the general life style of the family. And life styles may be reflected in part through the parents' values, interaction with their children, and their interests and activities outside the home. SCOPE asked how important parental aspirations are to the decision-making process, and to what extent students accept these aspirations as their own. Following the same line of thought, how do the occupations of the parents limit or enhance the occupational interests of their children?

Parental Expectations

The expectations that parents have for their children strongly influence many facets of students' lives. Among those that most concerned the SCOPE staff were the ways in which students perceive themselves, form peer relationships, assess school values, and make educational decisions.

What parents want for their children is not always made explicit, or their expectations may not be understood by the children. What school and career matters do students and parents talk over together? What values do students put on such conversations? Do students report that they get the most help from parents or from others?

By whatever means students become aware of parental expectations, it is important to know how students incorporate these expectations into their own plans and aspirations. By looking at related questions, it is possible to determine to what degree students share their parents' ideas about the importance of study, going to college, and competing for grades.

Self-Evaluation

The process of personal development is to a large degree generated by the day-to-day acts of self-evaluation, that is, the matching of one's own qualities with the qualities perceived in others, and the testing of conflicting possibilities against both external and internal standards. In reality, all attitudes, perceptions, and aspirations are expressions of self-evaluation. However, for this report, self-evaluation will be considered in more limited terms. Several aspects of self-evaluation in this more narrow sense were tapped in the questionnaires. Some items questioned the students directly about their ability, their general area of greatest competence, and their confidence about doing college work. Other items using a more indirect approach asked students to evaluate themselves through the eyes of others—their teachers, for example.

One of the major objective in analyzing this data was to assess the congruence between students' perceived strengths and their stated aspirations. How realistic are students' plans to go to college in light of their abilities? Is there a discrepancy between self-estimated college ability and students' perceptions of their teachers' evaluations of them? Which of the two is the better predictor of actual postsecondary choice?

Values

Students' educational and occupational aspirations cannot really be understood without knowing something about the values they hold.

Values reflect what people view as important in life. Values enable people to establish preferences among the wide array of interests and activities open to them. It should be found, therefore, that students' values will be crucial in the decision-making process.

Several sets of items in the questionnaires focused directly on values. For example, one series of items tested the importance of more general goals such as getting good grades, being a leader, pleasing parents. Another series tapped values through nonschool activities: for example, reading romance magazines, working for money, dating. Values were also probed by asking what one condition would give the respondent the most satisfaction in life.

In subsequent studies, the SCOPE staff will investigate several different kinds of questions about the influence of values in the decision-making process. For this report, questions asked how specific values are associated with particular educational and vocational choices. Do students who go to college really place more value on learning than those who don't go? Or is it more a matter of pleasing parents, keeping in step with friends, or making more money later on?

Perceptions of School

In the spring of 1966, SCOPE had a good opportunity to see how students who have nearly completed their high school careers viewed their experiences in school and how they might want to alter those experiences. Although the responses of students to such questions do not necessarily indicate weakness in the school curriculum, they are important indicators of student attitudes and perceptions of school. The project examined how these attitudes and perceptions influence students' decisions about postsecondary education.

Information-Seeking Activities

The sources of information that students use in exploring education and future work extend well beyond the family. To be sure, in American education the schools have increasingly assumed responsibility for guiding students' educational and career decisions. Not only do the resources differ among schools, but within any single school students vary in the ways in which they seek out these resources or are encouraged by school faculties to use them. For example, they may or may not seek the help of school counselors in attempting to clarify their educational and occupational aspirations, in selecting relevant courses of study, and in searching for financial aid for postsecondary education. In reference to these and other issues, some students may turn neither to home nor school but to other adults or to their peers.

SCOPE is concerned with the resources that students use in guiding their postsecondary choices. Do students seek information from colleges? Do students seek advice from persons other than their parents? Are students aware of resources available to them through college loans, bursaries, and scholarships? Do students value education to the extent that they will borrow money from their future income? SCOPE has been able to answer questions about the groups of students who use these various approaches in solving major questions regarding their educational futures.

Occupational Preferences

Results of other studies suggest that early occupational interests are poor predictors of actual occupational choice. Because of this unreliability, many studies have omitted early vocational interests in their investigations. Yet the unreliability of these early measures suggests the idea that actual occupational choice may represent a compromise between early fantasies and later realities. The position of the SCOPE staff is that the *process* of career development cannot really be understood without an analysis of the compromises that have been made, when and why they have occurred, and what students feel they have *lost,* as well as what they have gained, through each change in their aspirations. If educators are to understand what particular occupational and educational decisions lead to satisfying lives for some people but not for others, the importance of these early occupational interests must be recognized. Thus, portions of the questionnaires were devoted to questions about occupational preferences, although only a few of this data is reported here.

Intellectual Predisposition

A number of attitude items were presented to students at the June 1966 testing sessions. Although these items have been scored in order to provide several indicators about the way students respond to certain aspects of academic life, only an initial measure of "intellectual predisposition" has been used for this report. Related research at the Center for Research and Development in Higher Education and elsewhere has shown that intellectual disposition for college students is highly related to the type of institution selected, the choice of program, and persistence in college [Heist and Webster 1960 a&b]. A tentative scale, then, designed to indicate student differences in attitudes antecedent to intellectual orientation was adopted from the Omnibus Personality Inventory that had been developed at the Center. It was expected that students with high scores on the scale would demonstrate greater interest in and commitment to academic aspects of school life than would students with low scores. This scale has clearly differentiated students with different educational outcomes.

In contrast to the earlier profiles of the 1966 SCOPE seniors which were published in December of that year as a service to cooperating schools and colleges, this report seeks to answer questions about the relationships between selected characteristics of the students while in school and the types of institutions they might have entered after high school. It does anticipate the later transition from school to college of the second wave of SCOPE students who entered college in 1969–70. Many of the findings in this report invite new questions about the processes of decision-making during the school years. These are the questions to which the SCOPE longitudinal study of 1966–70 is addressed.

Chapter Three

Accessibility to Colleges

Freedom of choice is always limited by the number and nature of choices available. It may also be constrined by an infinitude of other factors, although the unbending parameters surrounding choice are the actual, the real, the viable options. To move the point from the abstract to the concrete, freedom of choice in higher education is limited by the number and nature of the institutions of higher education available.

The four states used in the SCOPE study (California, Illinois, Massachusetts, and North Carolina) have different schemes of higher education which set the outer limits to choice and which are necessary to understand before moving on to the less immutable and more personal determinants of the school-to-college decision-making process.

MASTER PLANS FOR HIGHER EDUCATION

Of the four states in the sample, California has the most highly structured master plan of higher education. By a 1960 amendment to the State Constitution, a tripartite structure of public higher education was created to include: (1) the two-year junior colleges, locally governed but under the general supervision of a state board of governors, offering standard collegiate courses, vocational-technical programs, and general liberal arts courses; (2) the state college system, governed by a board of trustees, providing college programs requiring more than three years, programs toward the mater's degree and, jointly with the University, the doctorate degree; and (3) the University of California, under a board of regents, providing education in the arts and sciences, having exclusive jurisdiction over training in the professions, having sole authority in public higher education for awarding the doctorate, and accepting primary responsibility in the state system for research. Admissions policy guidelines recommended that state colleges require freshmen to be in the top third and University freshmen in the top eighth of all graduates of California public high schools. Junior colleges are to admit any high school graduate or person over eighteen years of age who can be reasonably expected to profit from the instruction offered. The State Colleges and the University campuses were to shift from a 1960 ratio of fifty:fifty upper: lower division enrollment to a 1975 ratio of sixty:forty. Priority creation of more junior colleges was recommended, and to underwrite the shift of 50,000 lower division students to the junior colleges plus the expected growth spurt, state support of operating costs was to be increased from 30 percent to 45 percent by 1975, and state construction funds were to be allocated according to growth patterns. All state institutions of higher education were supposed to be tuition-free, but, in fact, only the junior colleges had little or no out-of-pocket fees at the time of enrollment [California State Department of Education 1960].

In Illinois, the Provisional Master Plan of 1964 called for the following: (1) the preservation of diversity among the state universities, the public two-year colleges, and the private colleges and universities; (2) a shift of enrollment from private to public institutions so that the 1963 figure of 53 percent would grow to 61 percent by 1975; and (3) two-year colleges to be removed from the realm and governance of the common schools and clearly made a part of higher education and given local administration while being under the general supervision of the Illinois Junior College Board. Junior colleges were to admit all qualified students wherever facilities permitted, while state universities would require applicants to have attained rank in the top half of their graduating high school class. Although the educational functions of the junior colleges were to be comprehensive, they were also held responsible for technical training and programs to aid under-educated adults. Meanwhile, state universities were instructed to emphasize upper division and graduate instruction and research. Fifty percent of the operating costs of the entire system was to be supplied by the state with construction costs to move in five years from a seventy-five:twenty-five ratio between state and local to a fifty:fifty ratio [Illinois Board of Higher Education 1964].

The direction of change in Massachusetts has been from heavy reliance on private institutions to increased public higher education. At present, the primary public institution is the University of Massachusetts, incorporated in 1863 and governed by an independent board of trustees. The nine state colleges are under the direct control of the State Board of Education. There are three technological institutes and the Maritime Academy, and, in 1966 when the data for this study was collected, there were ten junior colleges. The state only underwrites up to $100 per student toward making up half of any deficit in operating expenses. Massachusetts compares well with the nation in private education but ranks forty-eighth among the states in terms of state support for public institutions. By no semantic stretch could it be claimed that higher education is free. But, as noted, expansion of higher education in the public sector is being accelerated. Further, the 1957 Special Commission on Audit of State Needs recommended that there be immediate development of a statewide system of regional community colleges under the governance of the Board of Regional Community Colleges. The Board is charged with coordinating this system with the entire state higher educational program, with developing an overall plan and establishing institutions at suitable locations, and with seeing that an advisory board is created in each region to promote close cooperation between the area served and the community college [Massachusetts Legislature 1957].

North Carolina's system of higher education, like those in most states, has been established more in response to growing needs than by unified design. The University of North Carolina, established in 1789 and greatly expanded by normal growth and by a 1931 consolidation with two of the eleven public senior colleges, is the venerable keystone in the state system. There are nine remaining senior colleges, and in recent years five public community colleges and twenty industrial education centers have been established. North Carolina also has forty-five private institutions—one university, twenty-four senior colleges, sixteen junior colleges, and four religious schools. The 1962 Master Plan recognized increased enrollment needs and called for enrollment in public institutions to grow from 53 percent in 1960 to 62 percent by 1980. It called for a statewide board of higher education, overseeing the university with new campuses to meet new needs, and the expanded state college system which would incorporate three existing junior colleges. A unified system of public two-year commuter colleges was recommended, with the member colleges offering college parallel courses, technical-vocational programs, and adult education. Each institution will be governed by a local board of trustees but will be under the general supervision of the State Board of Education. The minimum of fifteen community colleges operational by 1965 were to make an open-door admissions policy a reality and by 1970 would care for one-fourth of all higher education enrollments. The open-door policy was mitigated somewhat by the financial formula of operating costs that called for 65 percent by state-federal funds, 15 percent by county taxpayers, and 20 percent by students [Planning Commission for North Carolina Higher Education 1962].

COUNTING THE COLLEGES

It is a truism that enrollment in colleges is highly dependent on availability of colleges. If colleges are available, students are likely to go; if they are not available, students are less likely to go. Trent and Medsker reported this in their 1968 study, *Beyond High School,* and the SCOPE data seems to substantiate this less-than-surprising finding. Primarily because of its early and

Table 3-1.   Postsecondary Institutions Available in the Four States in Fall, 1966

Type of Institution	California 190,000[a]	Illinois 78,000	Massachusetts 55,000	North Carolina 32,000
Public				
-2	–	–	1	–
2-4	74	18	11	3[b]
B.A.	6	–	4	7
M.A.	15	4	8	4
Ph.D.	11	4	2	4
Subtotal	106	26	26	18
Nonpublic				
Catholic				
-2	–	–	1	–
2-4	–	5	–	1
B.A.	9	11	13	1
M.A.	11	4	4	–
Ph.D.	–	3	2	–
Subtotal	20	23	20	2
Other Church-Related				
-2	–	–	–	–
2-4	1	2	–	12
B.A.	12	15	5	22
M.A.	11	12	–	1
Ph.D.	5	2	–	1
Subtotal	29	31	5	36
Independent				
-2[c]	1	2	5	1
2-4	2	8	16	2
B.A.	18	15	6	2
M.A.	11	12	17	–
Ph.D.	6	3	11	1
Subtotal	38	40	55	6
Total	193	120	106	62

Source: U.S. Department of Health, Education and Welfare, 1966-67.

[a]Estimated fall 1966 first-time students in all institutions for each state extrapolated from 1965/1968 data in American Council on Higher Education, 1969.

[b]The thirty-seven public technical institutes are not included here.

[c]Defined as Accredited Proprietary.

rapid development of community colleges and the regional availability of its public senior institutions, California offered opportunities in over 100 public colleges and universities. Massachusetts and Illinois supported twenty-six public institutions, and North Carolina, eighteen. Table 3-1 displays the number, degree levels, and type of control of institutions available in each of the four states in fall of 1966.[1]

Of course, the gross fact that California had more colleges than the other three states does not, by itself, demonstrate greater availability of colleges. A first look at related data suggests that Massachusetts had slightly higher availability. Taking California as the base of population comparison, we can see that in 1966 Massachusetts had 28 percent, Illinois had 57 percent, and North Carolina had 26 percent of California's population [U.S. Department of Health, Education and Welfare 1966–67]. Next, taking California as the base of first-time college enrollment, we see that in 1966 Massachusetts had 29 percent, Illinois had 41 percent, and North Carolina had 17 percent of California's first-time college enrollment [U.S. Department of Commerce 1967]. The ratios then of population:enrollment, still using California as the base, were California, 1:1; Massachusetts, 1:1.02; Illinois, 1:72; and North Carolina, 1:64.

This same pattern is suggested by two other comparisons. When the 1966 totals of first-time college enrollments are compared against the population category of eighteen- to forty-four year-olds (a census category that would include almost all college-goers), the percentages follow this descending order [American Council on Education 1967; U.S. Department of Commerce 1967]:

Massachusetts	.019
California	.018
Illinois	.013
North Carolina	.012

When the 1966 totals of first-time college enrollments are compared against the number of 1966 graduates of public and private high schools, the percentages follow the same descending order [Ibid.]:

Massachusetts	.71
California	.70
Illinois	.58
North Carolina	.48

1. Data on the number of institutions, their control, and their degree levels has derived from the *Education Directory*. The United States Office of Education was concerned with reporting certain kinds of institutions in the *Directory*. As a result, the figures do not include all institutions that were available, such as the thirty-seven technical institutes in North Carolina. These institutes offer a variety of programs ranging from short-term duration to full two-year programs. A number of similar kinds of institutions in the other three states were also outside the USOE interests, though some SCOPE students did enroll in them. However, the USOE listing does include the institutions in which the vast majority of the SCOPE students matriculated.

Table 3-2.   Extract from 1963 Study of Residence of First-Time Undergraduate Students in Four States

State	Number of Students from Other States	Percent of Out-of-State Students	Number of Resident Students Going to Other States	Percent of Resident Students Going to Other States
California	9,186	.06	7,585	.05
Illinois	5,894	.11	14,453	.23
Massachusetts	12,674	.35	7,143	.23
North Carolina	6,362	.29	1,961	.11

Source: Rice and Mason, 1965.

THE EFFECT OF STUDENT MIGRATION

The picture, though, may not be as clear as these comparisons would indicate. It could be blurred by the factor of in- and out-of-state attendance. A fall 1963 study, *Residence and Migration of College Students* [Rice and Mason 1965], reported these plus and minus balances of first-time undergraduate students in the four states sampled in SCOPE (see Table 3-2).

So, it appears that California lost to other states about the same percentage of students that it gained from other states. Illinois had a much higher percentage of students going out than coming in. Massachusetts had by far the highest percentage of in-migration but also sustained a 23 percent loss of young Massachusetts residents to colleges in other states. North Carolina also attracted a high percentage of students from other states but, unlike Massachusetts, did not lose a high percentage of its residents to colleges outside North Carolina.

The migration data on the 1966 SCOPE students entering college for the first time closely fits the pattern shown in Table 3-2. A rather low percentage of Californians and North Carolinians left their respective states, while a markedly higher percentage of Illinois and Massachusetts students left their home states to enter colleges elsewhere. This is presented in a detailed breakdown in Table 3-3.

Table 3-3. In- and Out-of-State Attendance of 1966 SCOPE Seniors at Public and Private Institutions

State		*In-State*			*Out-of-State*		
		Public	*Non-Public*	*Total*	*Public*	*Non-Public*	*Total*
California	N	3608	472	4080	129	185	314
	%	.82	.11	.93	.03	.04	.07
Illinois	N	2362	937	3299	395	744	1139
	%	.53	.21	.74	.09	.17	.26
Massachusetts	N	1431	1314	2745	211	612	823
	%	.40	.37	.77	.06	.17	.23
North Carolina	N	2693	1637	4330	151	312	463
	%	.56	.34	.90	.03	.07	.10
Four-State Totals	N	10094	4360	14454	886	1853	2739
	%	.70	.30	1.00	.32	.68	1.00

As can be seen in Table 3–3, almost one-fourth of the Illinois and Massachusetts students decided to attend colleges outside those two states, while in North Carolina and California 90 percent or more of their students opted for colleges in their own state. Certainly there are several factors operating to cause these different patterns. As later data will reveal, a high proportion of students migrating out of state are those with high achievement records and with affluent families. Certainly in Massachusetts the high-prestige, high-cost colleges and universities account for the high percentage of in-migration. Perhaps the most important single explanation of these differences lies in the availability of public, low-cost institutions. The public two-year segment accounts for a considerable portion of student retention in each state, particularly in California. North Carolina's private two-year and four-year liberal arts institutions, on the other hand, appear to account for a greater share of its holding power when compared with comparable institutions in the other SCOPE states.

The contrasts among the states of the proportion of SCOPE college-goers who selected a public institution is quite marked. California's 82 percent is considerably higher than any other state and reflects a history of public over private education in that state. The fact that nearly 73 percent of the enrollments in public colleges were in the comprehensive, tuition-free community colleges is particularly noteworthy. Massachusetts, by comparison, demonstrates a higher holding power than the other states by its nonpublic institutions which attracted 37 percent of the college attenders. These students were concentrated primarily in the Catholic liberal arts colleges and the independent university-level institutions. North Carolina also retained 34 percent of its college-goers in nonpublic institutions, and these seemed to cluster in two-year and liberal arts colleges which were under the control of denominations other than Catholic.

The out-migration patterns also give rise to speculation about the characteristics of the students who have decided to leave the state for post-secondary education. It is possible, for example, that certain types of institutions are skimming highly select students from the upper levels of academic ability, thus causing a "brain drain" for some states.

To provide diverse colleges and more of them to the diverse student population certainly seemed to be the motivating thrust of the master plans for higher education in the four states. They express a conclusion voiced by Warren Willingham in his *Free-Access Higher Education:* "Accelerating public expectations now demands that equal opportunity for relevant education beyond high school is a right not a privilege" [1970, p. 228]. These master plans are predicated on the proposition that more and diverse colleges attract more and diverse students. The data from SCOPE and other studies substantiates the essential validity of this proposition, although the complexity of factors involved and the different levels of progress toward equal opportunity make this substantiation much clearer in California than in the other states. One way to explore this issue further is to see what happens at that first branching where some continue on to the college world and others veer off to the noncollege world.

Chapter Four

First Branchings

If a study were to be made of the entire life span of a group of people, the maps of their lives would be marked with crucial either-or decisions which would chart the directional zigs and zags that each life took. One of these crossroads in American society occurs at high school graduation when young people are obliged to take either the college route or the noncollege route. This is not to imply that the decision is made precisely at this fork in the road nor should it be inferred that the decision is always irrevocable. However, leaving high school is the time when a decision is acted out, and if the person goes far enough down one road it is difficult for him to back up and go the other way. This is when a massive separation takes place, and it should be interesting to find how many go one way and how many go the other, what the distinguishing factors are between the two groups, and what the secondary branchings are within each group.

THE FIFTY:FIFTY SPLIT

In the spring of 1966 an array of information pertaining to decision-making was collected on 33,965 high school seniors in four states, the first sample of a total of 80,007 secondary students to be included in SCOPE's longitudinal study of access to postsecondary education. One year later, in the spring of 1967, the students in this first wave who had gone to college were located. It was found that the 1966 graduating classes from the four project states split nearly equally into two groups, one of which had been pulled into the college world and the other drawn into what might be considered a world of instant adulthood [Keniston 1966].

In gross terms for the four states combined, 50.7 percent of the 1966 twelfth graders were in some postsecondary institution in 1967, 47.6 percent had not gone on to further education, and 1.7 percent were nonrespondents. Although no claim is made that the four-state composite constitutes a national sample, this split nearly replicates the national norms for college-going in 1966 [U.S. Department of Commerce 1967].

Composites, like averages, can obscure differences that should be noted. Figure 4-1 reveals differing patterns of college attendance for each of the SCOPE states. These figures show that the youngest state in the study, California, and the oldest state, Massachusetts, sent 58 percent and 56 percent, respectively, of their graduates on to some postsecondary education. However, there are indications that quite dissimilar forces were at work in producing similar results in states which historically have markedly different approaches to public and private education. State differences in college-going are also shown by the data for Illinois where 51 percent of the graduates in this study went on, and North Carolina where 42 percent of the SCOPE students entered a postsecondary institution.

DIFFERENCES BY STATE

So, some graduates went to college and some did not, and there are some differences among states—but these are only the most gross discriminations for each of the two groups. Within each state, students who went to college distributed themselves across a complex pattern of institutions. For the purpose at

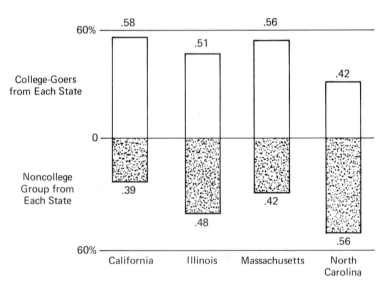

Figure 4-1. Comparison by State of College Group and Noncollege Group of 1966 SCOPE Seniors[a]

[a]Does not include "no response" answers.

hand, these institutions have been classified by degree level (viz., less than two years; two years–less than four years; four years; more than four years–master's degree; and more than four years–doctorate). Further, these different institutions are under either public or private control, with the private colleges reported as either Catholic, Other Denominations, or Independent. Some of the differences in the characteristics of students attending publicly and privately controlled institutions will be highlighted later in this report, including the quite selective attraction of the independent universities and colleges. To tell the story of selection and differentiation, the data will be organized and presented by degree level, by control, or by combining these two classifications.

Although there are great similarities in the way students from each of the project states distributed themselves across institutions, the data also shows that students in the four states tend to use the several types of institutions available to them in proportionately different wasy. For example, a much higher percentage of boys than girls attend Ph.D.-granting institutions in Massachusetts, and a larger percentage of both sexes attend community colleges in California than in any of the other three states. In view of the availability of a community college within commuting distance of nearly 90 percent of the youth of California,[1] it is not surprising to note that 35 percent of California twelfth graders went on to a two-year college while less than half that percentage made such a choice in any of the other three states. Furthermore, California students had a range of choices among colleges that were low in cost and close to home [Willingham 1970].

SCOPE students who were not located in college were subdivided on the basis of their response to an item in the twelfth grade questionnaire which asked about their posthigh-school plans. Thus, there are two quite different groups of students who did *not* go to college after graduation: those who *did not plan* to go to college while in high school and, in fact, *did not* go; and those who *did plan* to go on but *did not* attend college. Table 4–1 makes the separation between those who went to college and those who did not and then gives the number and percentage of those who fell into the subdivisions of the two categories just described.

Within the noncollege category the state differences are immediately obvious. California has a considerably lower proportion of the "no college:did-not-plan-to-go" graduates than any of the other states: 20 percent of the state sample of 7,567. In contrast, nearly one-third of the 11,377 North Carolina

---

1. Warren Willingham, in *Free-Access Higher Education* [1970] contends that "Throughout the state 60 percent of the population lives within commuting distance of a free-access college." In their 1969 *Study of Additional Centers,* the Coordinating Council of Higher Education stoutly defends the figure of 90 percent within commuting distance. The difference, of course, follows from how "commuting distance" is defined. Since the definition of the Coordinating Council is an operational one used in planning throughout California, their figure of 90 percent is used for the purpose at hand.

Table 4-1. Number and Percentage in Each Postsecondary Outcome of 1966 SCOPE Seniors (by State)

State		No College		College					No Response	Total
		Did Not Plan To Go	Did Plan To Go	Degree Level of Institutions						
				Less Than 2 Years	2 Years, Less Than 4 Years	4 Years B.A.	More Than 4 Years M.A.	More Than 4 Years Ph.D.		
California	N	1538	1394	124	2672	128	703	770	238	7567
	%	.20	.19	.02	.35	.02	.09	.10	.03	1.00
Illinois	N	2564	1628	110	1368	514	1188	1264	50	8686
	%	.28	.19	.01	.16	.06	.14	.15	.01	1.00
Massachusetts	N	1728	938	160	1035	582	733	1064	95	6335
	%	.27	.15	.03	.16	.09	.12	.17	.01	1.00
North Carolina	N	3740	2638	278	1582	1163	791	979	206	11377
	%	.33	.23	.02	.14	.10	.07	.09	.02	1.00
Four-State Totals	N	9570	6598	672	6657	2387	3415	4077	589	33965
	%	.28	.19	.02	.20	.07	.10	.12	.02	1.00

sample did not go on and, while still in high school, said they did not plan to continue their education. The groups that planned to continue education beyond high school but did not go do not reflect such sharp state differences, even though there is approximately an eight-point spread between the Massachusetts low of 15 percent and the North Carolina high of 23 percent.

The college-goers follwed the pattern of accessibility characteristic of their state. California, with 74 community colleges in 1966, had 35 percent of its sample enroll in the two-year colleges. Massachusetts, noted for its private and prestigious universities, had 29 percent of its sample enroll in the combined M.A.- and Ph.D.-granting institutions. The bachelor's degree, once the norm, is no longer the terminal degree in most colleges. California and Illinois, which emphasized public university development under the land-grant college movement, had very few students enrolled in four-year, liberal arts colleges. Even Massachusetts and North Carolina, where the four-year colleges have had historical importance, had 10 percent or less of their respective 1966 samples enroll in such institutions. As a matter of fact, Table 4-1 reveals that enrollment by degree level of insitution follows a bi-modal curve, with one crest at the junior college, a trough at the four-year college, and the second apex at the M.A.- and Ph.D.-granting institutions.

DIFFERENCES BY SEX

Slightly more girls than boys finish high school [U.S. Department of Commerce 1967]. However, when the graduating seniors divide into the college and the noncollege streams, the college stream swells with more boys. This sex difference is true in each of the four states, though more noticeably so in Illinois and Massachusetts. The difference between one state and another in percentage of college enrollment is greater than the difference between one sex and the other, e.g., California at 58 percent versus North Carolina at 42 percent is much larger than the biggest sex difference, 55 percent versus 47 percent found in Illinois. The point here is that although sex is a factor in the basic decision between college and noncollege, it seems to be a factor that fluctuates in a manner constant with other determinants. The detailed facts on differences by sex and by state are presented in Table 4-2.

These state differences are further accentuated by the dissimilar pattern for girls and boys shown by detailed subdivisions in Table 4-3. California's "no-plan" students show similar outcomes for boys and girls, although more girls than boys who planned to go failed to matriculate. This same pattern, but with much higher percentages, is found in North Carolina. The most marked sex differences among the noncollege group are found in the Illinois and Massachusetts "no-plan" subdivision where, in each case, nearly 8 percent more girls than boys did not plan to enter some postsecondary education program.

State and sex differences are just as apparent among the category of

Table 4-2.   Comparison by Sex and by State of Number and
Percentage of 1966 SCOPE Seniors in College and Not in College

State			In College	Not In College	No Response	Total
California	M	N	2252	1420	142	3814
		%	.59	.37	.04	1.00
	F	N	2145	1512	96	3753
		%	.57	.40	.03	1.00
	T	N	4397	2932	238	7567
		%	.58	.39	.03	1.00
Illinois	M	N	2361	1871	41	4273
		%	.55	.44	.01	1.00
	F	N	2083	2321	9	4413
		%	.47	.52	.01	1.00
	T	N	4444	4192	50	8686
		%	.51	.48	.01	1.00
Massachusetts	M	N	1896	1256	47	3199
		%	.59	.39	.02	1.00
	F	N	1678	1410	48	3136
		%	.53	.45	.02	1.00
	T	N	3574	2666	95	6335
		%	.56	.42	.02	1.00
North Carolina	M	N	2362	2995	124	5481
		%	.43	.55	.02	1.00
	F	N	2431	3383	82	5896
		%	.41	.57	.02	1.00
	T	N	4793	6738	206	11377
		%	.42	.56	.02	1.00
Four-State Totals	M	N	8871	7542	354	16767
		%	.53	.45	.02	1.00
	F	N	8337	8626	235	17198
		%	.48	.50	.02	1.00
	T	N	17208	16168	589	33965
		%	.51	.47	.02	1.00

Note.   This data includes college students who were located *in* and *out* of state of high
school attendance. Because of the rigor of follow-up, it is assumed that nonlocated students
were not in college in 1966-67.

Table 4-3. Number and Percentage in Each Postsecondary Outcome of 1966 SCOPE Seniors (by Sex and by State)

State		No College		College — Degree Level of Institutions					No Response	Total
		Did Not Plan To Go	Did Plan To Go	Less Than 2 Years	2 Years, Less Than 4 Years	4 Years B.A.	More Than 4 Years M.A.	More Than 4 Years Ph.D.		
California										
M	N	787	633	4	1504	54	341	347	142	3814
	%	.21	.17	.01	.39	.01	.09	.09	.04	1.00
F	N	751	761	120	1168	72	362	423	96	3753
	%	.20	.20	.03	.31	.02	.10	.11	.03	1.00
Illinois										
M	N	1089	782	21	772	273	531	764	41	4273
	%	.26	.18	.01	.18	.06	.12	.18	.01	1.00
F	N	1475	846	89	596	241	657	500	9	4413
	%	.33	.19	.02	.14	.05	.15	.11	.01	1.00
Massachusetts										
M	N	757	499	29	522	276	332	737	47	3199
	%	.24	.16	.09	.16	.09	.11	.23	.02	1.00
F	N	971	439	131	513	306	401	327	48	3136
	%	.31	.14	.04	.16	.10	.13	.10	.02	1.00
North Carolina										
M	N	1835	1160	63	820	530	360	589	124	5481
	%	.33	.21	.01	.15	.10	.07	.11	.02	1.00
F	N	1905	1478	215	762	633	431	390	82	5896
	%	.32	.25	.04	.13	.11	.07	.07	.01	1.00
Four-State Totals										
M	N	4468	3074	117	3618	1135	1564	2437	354	16767
	%	.27	.18	.01	.22	.07	.09	.14	.02	1.00
F	N	5102	3524	555	3039	1252	1851	1640	235	17198
	%	.30	.20	.03	.18	.07	.11	.10	.01	1.00

college-goers as in the noncollege category. It has already been noted that California boys and girls used the community college much more than students in the other states. Moreover, more boys (39 percent) than girls (31 percent) attended the California two-year institutions. This sex difference was also true in Illinois where 18 percent of the boys entered the community college, as compared with only 14 percent of the girls. California was the only state of the four in which more girls than boys attended the M.A.- and Ph.D.-granting colleges and universities. Approximately 7 percent more boys from Illinois and 13 percent from Massachusetts used the Ph.D.-level universities than did girls. The heavier attendance of boys at the junior college and the Ph.D.-granting university level in these states may be the result, in part, of the higher proportion of girls using the M.A.-level colleges which tend to be teacher preparation institutions. It may also be explained by the much higher proportion of Illinois and Massachusetts girls who neither planned to go nor did in fact go to college. The Massachusetts pattern is noteworthy because it shows the greatest difference in Ph.D.-level attendance between boys (23 percent) and girls (10 percent) among the four states.

At first branching, then, the gross fact is that slightly more than half of high school graduates go to college and slightly less than half do not. First refinements of this gross fact reveal a pattern of differences from state to state that is congruent with the accessibility of higher education in each state. A closer look also shows marked differences by sex, with more boys than girls planning to go and actually going to college. When the dichotomy of college versus noncollege gets further subdivided and therefore made more discriminating, the variance both by state and by sex becomes much more evident. So, the determinants' state (educational system within a geographic area) and sex have been introduced but will be brought up again in new contexts. Attention will be turned next to student perceptions and attitudes as they affect decision-making.

Chapter Five

Student Perceptions and Attitudes

To a degree that is hard to measure but easy to see, many life decisions are prophecies that are self-fulfilled. The boy whose "old blue" father sends in his son's application to Yale on the day the son is born ends up going to Yale. Youngsters who grow up in intellectually disposing environments develop intellectual predispositions which, in turn, become determinants in their levels of educational aspiration. Students in high school who expect themselves to go to college meet their own self-expectations.

These statements have a ring of common sense, perhaps even sound like truisms, but when subjected to the test of evidence often require hedging and qualifying. Even so, the data to be presented will corroborate the more cautious conclusions of other research on the potent influence of mothers and fathers in student decision-making about education [Simpson 1962; Trent and Medsker 1968; Kandel and Lesser 1969]. In this chapter, the exploration of student perceptions and attitudes will reveal that although fulfillment of expectations is indeed there, it is not nearly as inevitable or faithful as common sense suggests.

STUDENT PERCEPTION OF
PARENTAL ASPIRATIONS

In 1966, the SCOPE seniors were asked what level of postsecondary education, if any, their parents expected them to attain. Their responses echoed the American dream: the new generation, particularly the new male generation, will go to college and thereby reap the benefits that supposedly accrue. In actual fact, although 48 percent of these seniors did not go to any form of postsecondary school, 80 percent or more of them reported that their parents expected them to go to some form of college. With some variance by state, about 50 percent of the students thought their parents expected them to finish college or even work

31

for a master's or a doctorate degree. These first gross comparisons are given in Table 5-1. Note that California and Massachusetts parents are perceived as having slightly higher educational aspirations for their children and that North Carolina parents are perceived as being less ambitious for their children to secure a B.A. or do postgraduate work. Also note that in all four states the perceived aspirations above that of "High School Only" approached or exceeded 80 percent. Of course, the higher the perceived parental aspiration level, the higher the potential for perceived failure. It is depressing to speculate upon how many of the youngsters who did not go to college saw themselves as losers, as disappointments to their parents, and as disappointments to themselves.

Table 5-2 gives a much more refined picture: one of parental aspirations as perceived by the 1966 SCOPE seniors compared with the level of postsecondary institution, if any, in which the students actually enrolled. It should be noted that the entry institution does not necessarily indicate how long a student will stay in college. For example, a Ph.D. might start his collegiate education in a junior college. There is, however, a strong positive relationship between the type of entry institution and the expected level of educational achievement. The percentage figures in Table 5-2 are worth close examination because they tell a significant story. The youngsters who did not plan to go to college and who, in fact, did not go, saw their parents as having minimal educational ambitions for them. (About 80 percent or more of this group in each of the four states responded that their parents would be content if they finished high school or perhaps a year or so of college.) On the other hand, the youngsters who entered four-year colleges or universities saw their parents as fully expecting them to earn college degrees. (From 86 to 94 percent of this group in each of the four states responded that their parents expected them to garner a B.A. degree or more.) Note how in every state about 50 percent or more (62 percent in California) of the students who enrolled in junior colleges perceived their parents as expecting them to transfer to an upper division college to secure a B.A. degree or better. Is it any wonder that two-thirds of junior college students classify themselves as transfer students [Medsker and Tillery 1971]?

In Table 5-2, the similarities among the states overshadow the

Table 5-1. Parents' Educational Aspirations for Their Children as Perceived by SCOPE Seniors

State	High School Only	Some College	B.A. or Postgraduate	Total[a]
California	.14	.29	.54	.97
Illinois	.21	.27	.49	.97
Massachusetts	.19	.25	.55	.99
North Carolina	.19	.34	.44	.97

[a]Does not include "don't know" responses.

Table 5–2. Parents' Educational Aspirations for Their Children as Perceived by SCOPE Seniors (N = 33,149) with Different Postsecondary Outcomes (by State)

Parents' Educational Aspirations for Children

Postsecondary Outcomes		H.S. Only	Some Coll	4-Yr Grad	Post-Grad	Total[a]
		California				
No College	No Plan To Go	.46	.32	.13	.04	.95
	Planned To Go	.08	.45	.35	.08	.96
Special Schools		.15	.71	.10	.04	1.00
Junior Colleges[b]		.05	.30	.52	.10	.97
Senior Colleges		.02	.08	.70	.18	.98
All Students		.14	.29	.44	.10	.97
		Massachusetts				
No College	No Plan To Go	.55	.30	.10	.02	.97
	Planned To Go	.12	.42	.37	.06	.97
Special Schools		.08	.71	.14	.05	.98
Junior Colleges[b]		.03	.40	.50	.06	.99
Senior Colleges		.02	.04	.75	.18	.99
All Students		.19	.25	.46	.09	.99
		Illinois				
No College	No Plan To Go	.57	.29	.08	.02	.96
	Planned To Go	.12	.47	.33	.06	.98
Special Schools		.11	.77	.10	.02	1.00
Junior Colleges[b]		.05	.33	.48	.11	.97
Senior Colleges		.02	.09	.70	.16	.97
All Students		.21	.27	.40	.09	.97
		North Carolina				
No College	No Plan To Go	.47	.35	.10	.04	.96
	Planned To Go	.11	.53	.27	.07	.98
Special Schools		.07	.74	.16	.02	1.00
Junior Colleges[b]		.04	.46	.43	.06	.99
Senior Colleges		.01	.05	.77	.17	1.00
All Students		.19	.34	.36	.08	.97

[a] Does not include "don't know" responses.
[b] Defined as two years, less than four years.

Table 5-3. Parents' Educational Aspirations for Their Children as Perceived by SCOPE Seniors with Different Postsecondary Outcomes (by State and by Sex)

| Postsecondary Outcomes | | Parents' Educational Aspirations for Children | | | | | | | | | |
| | | California | | | | | Illinois | | | | |
		H.S. Only	Some Coll	4-Yr Grad	Post-Grad	Total[a]	H.S. Only	Some Coll	4-Yr Grad	Post-Grad	Total[a]
No College	No Plan To Go										
	M	.42	.25	.20	.06	.93	.51	.28	.13	.03	.95
	F	.49	.39	.06	.03	.93	.62	.29	.05	.01	.97
	Planned To Go										
	M	.09	.32	.44	.12	.97	.10	.33	.45	.09	.97
	F	.08	.56	.28	.05	.97	.13	.59	.22	.03	.97
Special Schools	M	.00	1.00	.00	.00	1.00	.24	.62	.10	.05	1.00
	F	.15	.71	.10	.04	1.00	.08	.81	.10	.01	1.00
Junior Colleges[b]	M	.05	.20	.58	.13	.96	.05	.24	.53	.14	.96
	F	.05	.42	.45	.05	.97	.06	.45	.42	.01	.94
Senior Colleges	M	.02	.02	.64	.29	.97	.02	.04	.67	.25	.98
	F	.01	.13	.75	.09	.97	.03	.15	.73	.06	.98
All Students	M	.13	.20	.49	.15	.97	.17	.20	.46	.14	.97
	F	.14	.38	.39	.05	.96	.25	.34	.35	.04	.98

		Massachusetts					North Carolina				
No College											
No Plan To Go	M	.40	.26	.17	.02	.93	.48	.30	.14	.04	.96
	F	.60	.33	.05	.01	.99	.46	.41	.06	.04	.97
Planned To Go	M	.10	.33	.46	.08	.97	.13	.45	.33	.07	.98
	F	.13	.54	.28	.03	.98	.09	.59	.23	.07	.98
Special Schools	M	.03	.59	.28	.03	.93	.06	.75	.17	.00	.98
	F	.09	.73	.11	.05	.98	.08	.74	.16	.02	1.00
Junior Colleges[b]	M	.03	.31	.58	.06	.98	.05	.40	.47	.06	.98
	F	.02	.48	.41	.07	.98	.04	.52	.38	.05	.99
Senior Colleges	M	.02	.02	.70	.25	.99	.01	.03	.73	.23	1.00
	F	.05	.06	.82	.04	.97	.01	.07	.81	.10	.99
All Students	M	.15	.18	.51	.13	.97	.20	.28	.39	.10	.97
	F	.22	.31	.40	.05	.98	.19	.40	.34	.06	.99

[a] Does not include "don't know" responses.
[b] Defined as two years, less than four years.

Table 5-4. Postsecondary Outcomes Compared with Parental Educational Aspirations as Perceived by SCOPE Seniors

Parental Educational Aspiration Levels	Postsecondary Outcomes				
	No College		Special Schools	Junior College	Senior College
	No Plan To Go	Planned To Go			
	90%				
High School Only	.79	.11	.01	.05	.03
Some College	.31	.32	.05	.24	.06
				77%	
4-Year Graduate	.07	.15	.06	.24	.53
				74%	
Postgraduate	.10	.15	.01	.19	.55

differences. This may be somewhat misleading, however, since some differences may be obscured by the collapsing of data into composite percentages. One such possible difference in parental aspiration is the factor of sex. Parents expect their sons to get more education than their daughters or, at least, that is how the sons and daughters interpret it. Comparison of the male/female percentages in each of the columns and rows in Table 5-3 helps to clarify those differences that are perceived.

Except in the case of North Carolina, the first column, "High School Only," shows a tendency for youngsters to think their parents are more willing to see daughters than sons quit at the end of high school. The second column, "Some College," clearly reveals that parents are seen as being more content to see girls than boys limit their higher education to one or two years. In column 3, "4-Year Grad," the message is more ambiguous but can be decoded to read that parents whose children do not make it into a four-year college or university have higher expectations (greater disappointment?) for their sons than for their daughters. But this does not apply to the youngsters who do matriculate to a four-year college or university. For this group, the aspiration level is higher for girls than for boys. Perhaps the middle and upper classes, who populate the universities in disproportionate numbers, are more liberated in their views of sex role. And, as is certainly true in North Carolina and Illinois, the four-year colleges often specialize in teacher preparation and, therefore, tend to cater to women. Note, however, how perceived parental aspiration changes for this group in column 4, "Post Grad": once again, more parents expect the males to earn the master's degrees and the doctorate degrees and the other postgraduate tickets to "success."

So far this question has been asked: What were the parental educational aspirations of SCOPE students in the five categories of outcome? The question can also be asked the other way: What were the categories of postsecondary outcome for each of the four levels of parental educational aspirations? These are not reciprocals although the answers that come through tend to corroborate each other. Of the students who reported that their parents expected them to attain the B.A. degree or go beyond the four-year degree, about 75 percent were enrolled in means toward that end, i.e., junior colleges, colleges, and universities. On the other hand, of those students who reported that their parents did not expect them to go beyond high school, 90 percent did not enroll in any postsecondary institution. This is shown in composite form in Table 5-4.

There are enough variations of these percentage figures by state and by sex to warrant the detailed breakdown presented in Table 5-5. In California, students who reported their parents as having only high school ambitions for them were not as inclined to accept their parents' low expectation. Of this group, 16 percent of the California boys and 12 percent of the California girls entered a junior college. These percentages are significantly higher than the equivalent percentages for the other three states. Note also that California boys who think that their parents want them to get a B.A. degree or an M.A. or Ph.D. degree are twice as likely to begin their college work in a junior college than their counterparts in the other three states. This same fact on entry obtains for the California girls, except that the difference with the other three states is almost twice again as high for the girls whose parents expect them to get an M.A. or Ph.D. In all states, among students enrolled in four-year colleges or universities, there was a higher percentage of girls than boys who reported that their parents wanted them to get a B.A. degree, but a higher percentage of boys than girls who reported that their parents expected them to go beyond the baccalaureate to a master's degree or doctorate.

STUDENT ASPIRATIONS AND OUTCOMES

There are some sidelight congruities between student aspirations and outcomes beyond the central focus of whether students who aspired to college actually went. By a vast majority, students who said they wanted to go to public institutions went to public colleges and universities. There was a similar congruence between aspirations and outcome for those who preferred private institutions. As to size of institution, students going to public institutions were not averse to large numbers, while students who went to private universities were about equally divided in preference for large and small institutions. In contrast, those SCOPE seniors who ended up in non-Catholic, church-related colleges overwhelmingly preferred small colleges.

The central focus was, of course, on the educational aspirations the students had for themselves. When data on student aspiration was compared with data on perceived parental aspiration, the congruence was striking. The similarity

Table 5-5. Postsecondary Outcomes Compared with Parents' Educational Aspirations for Their Children as Perceived by SCOPE Seniors (by State and by Sex)

		Postsecondary Outcomes											
		California						Illinois					
		No College						No College					
Parental Educational Aspirations		No Plan To Go	Did Plan To Go	Spec Schls	Jr Coll[b]	Sr Coll	Total[a]	No Plan To Go	Did Plan To Go	Spec Schls	Jr Coll[b]	Sr Coll	Total[a]
High School Only	M	.69	.11	.00	.16	.03	.99	.79	.12	.01	.05	.03	1.00
	F	.73	.11	.04	.12	.02	1.00	.82	.10	.01	.03	.04	1.00
Some College	M	.28	.28	.01	.42	.02	1.00	.37	.31	.02	.22	.08	1.00
	F	.21	.31	.06	.35	.08	1.00	.29	.34	.05	.18	.14	1.00
4-Year Graduate	M	.09	.16	.00	.48	.27	1.00	.07	.18	.00	.21	.53	.99
	F	.03	.15	.01	.36	.45	1.00	.05	.12	.01	.16	.66	1.00
Post Graduate	M	.08	.14	.00	.37	.41	1.00	.05	.12	.00	.18	.65	1.00
	F	.11	.21	.03	.30	.37	1.00	.11	.14	.01	.23	.51	1.00
All Students	M	.21	.17	.00	.41	.20	.99	.26	.19	.00	.18	.37	1.00
	F	.21	.21	.03	.32	.23	1.00	.34	.19	.02	.14	.32	1.00

		Massachusetts						North Carolina					
High School Only	M	.79	.11	.00	.04	.03	.97	.80	.14	.00	.04	.01	.99
	F	.85	.09	.02	.02	.03	1.00	.82	.12	.01	.03	.01	.99
Some College	M	.34	.29	.03	.29	.03	.98	.37	.35	.03	.22	.03	1.00
	F	.34	.25	.01	.26	.06	.92	.34	.38	.07	.17	.04	1.00
4-Year Graduate	M	.08	.14	.01	.19	.58	1.00	.12	.18	.01	.18	.51	1.00
	F	.04	.10	.01	.17	.68	1.00	.06	.18	.02	.15	.60	1.00
Post Graduate	M	.04	.10	.00	.07	.79	1.00	.15	.15	.00	.09	.61	1.00
	F	.08	.09	.04	.22	.56	.99	.19	.29	.01	.10	.41	1.00
All Students	M	.24	.16	.01	.17	.43	1.00	.34	.22	.01	.15	.28	1.00
	F	.32	.14	.04	.17	.33	1.00	.33	.25	.04	.13	.25	1.00

[a]Does not include "don't know" responses.
[b]Defined as two years, less than four years.

Table 5-6. Educational Aspirations Reported by SCOPE Seniors and Compared with Student Perception of Parental Aspirations

State	Students' (Parents') Educational Aspirations		
	High School Only	*Some College*	*B.A. or Postgraduate*
California	.14 (.14)[a]	.32 (.29)[a]	.51 (.54)[a]
Illinois	.19 (.21)	.27 (.27)	.51 (.49)
Massachusetts	.18 (.19)	.25 (.25)	.54 (.55)
North Carolina	.19 (.19)	.36 (.34)	.42 (.44)

[a]Percentage figures for perceived parental aspirations.

was close enough to suggest that perceived parental aspirations were really projections of the students' own aspirations. Or, perhaps, that children ingest the expectations their parents have for them. The small differences between the two sets of data certainly contradict any notion that students perceive their parents as holding them to a much higher educational expectancy than they hold themselves. Table 5-6 reports, by state, the gross percentage of students falling into the three broad aspiration categories of "High School Only," "Some College," and "B.A. or Postgraduate" and compares these with the equivalent percentages for perceived parental aspirations. Again, 78 percent or more (83 percent in California) of the students said that they would like to go to some postsecondary institution and, again, with North Carolina the exception, over 50 percent of the students said they would like to finish college or even do postgraduate studies. As will be shown shortly, the dream is better than reality; the aspiration is higher than the outcome.

Collapsing data, as was done in Table 5-6, sometimes irons out differences that should be noted. The striking fact remains that the educational aspirations students hold for themselves and the educational aspirations the students think their parents hold for them are remarkably similar. But as Table 5-7 shows, students who enrolled in junior colleges thought that their parents aspired more than the students did to their getting a B.A. degree. The same difference obtained among students who actually enrolled in four-year colleges or universities. In both cases, as can be seen by comparing Table 5-7 with Table 5-2, the explanation has a reverse twist; yes, the percentages of junior and senior college students aspiring to "4-Year Degree" is less than that of parents because, in every state, a higher percentage of students than parents aspired to "More than 4-Year Degree." This probably reflects a generation gap in perception: the parents see the B.A. as the entry ticket the way it was in the 1940s, while their children see that the ante has been upped to an M.A. or Ph.D. Table 5-7 again demonstrates that students who enter junior colleges do

Table 5-7. Educational Aspirations of SCOPE Seniors (N = 33,159) with Different Postsecondary Outcomes (by State)

		Students' Educational Aspirations								
		California					Illinois			
Postsecondary Outcomes		H.S. Only	Some Coll	4-Yr Grad	Post-Grad	Total[a]	H.S. Only	Some Coll	4-Yr Grad	Post-Grad	Total[a]
No College	No Plan To Go	.51	.30	.08	.03	.92	.57	.28	.07	.02	.94
	Planned To Go	.06	.51	.28	.13	.98	.06	.52	.30	.10	.98
Special Schools		.10	.80	.03	.04	.97	.06	.80	.11	.02	.99
Junior Colleges[b]		.03	.35	.44	.14	.96	.03	.36	.41	.17	.97
Senior Colleges		.01	.07	.60	.32	1.00	.01	.07	.62	.28	.98
All Students		.14	.32	.36	.15	.97	.19	.27	.36	.15	.97

		Massachusetts					North Carolina			
Postsecondary Outcomes		H.S. Only	Some Coll	4-Yr Grad	Post-Grad	Total[a]	H.S. Only	Some Coll	4-Yr Grad	Post-Grad	Total[a]
No College	No Plan To Go	.56	.26	.08	.02	.92	.50	.34	.07	.03	.94
	Planned To Go	.07	.47	.34	.10	.98	.07	.57	.27	.09	1.00
Special Schools		.10	.73	.07	.09	.99	.07	.79	.11	.02	.99
Junior Colleges[b]		.02	.43	.44	.09	.98	.04	.50	.35	.09	.98
Senior Colleges		.01	.05	.62	.31	.99	.01	.06	.66	.26	.99
All Students		.18	.25	.38	.16	.97	.19	.36	.31	.11	.97

[a] Does not include "don't know" responses.
[b] Defined as two years, less than four years.

Table 5-8. Educational Aspirations of SCOPE Seniors with Different Postsecondary Outcomes (by State and by Sex)

Postsecondary Outcomes			California					Illinois				
		H.S. Only	Some Coll	4-Yr Grad	Post-Grad	Total[a]	H.S. Only	Some Coll	4-Yr Grad	Post-Grad	Total[a]
No College	No Plan To Go	M	.47	.26	.12	.04	.89	.54	.28	.09	.02	.93
		F	.54	.34	.04	.02	.94	.59	.29	.05	.01	.94
	Planned To Go	M	.07	.40	.33	.17	.97	.07	.41	.37	.13	.98
		F	.05	.60	.24	.09	.98	.05	.62	.24	.08	.99
Special Schools		M	.00	1.00	.00	.00	1.00	.10	.71	.19	.00	1.00
		F	.10	.80	.03	.04	.97	.06	.82	.09	.02	.99
Junior Colleges[b]		M	.03	.27	.48	.17	.95	.03	.28	.43	.23	.97
		F	.03	.46	.39	.09	.97	.03	.46	.40	.10	.99
Senior Colleges		M	.01	.03	.48	.45	.97	.01	.04	.55	.38	.98
		F	.01	.09	.69	.20	.99	.01	.11	.69	.17	.98
All Students		M	.13	.24	.38	.20	.95	.16	.22	.37	.21	.96
		F	.14	.39	.34	.10	.97	.21	.33	.34	.09	.97

Students' Educational Aspirations

		Massachusetts					*North Carolina*				
No College No Plan To Go	M	.52	.22	.14	.02	.90	.51	.29	.10	.03	.93
	F	.60	.29	.04	.02	.95	.49	.39	.04	.03	.95
College Planned To Go	M	.07	.37	.41	.13	.98	.09	.50	.32	.09	1.00
	F	.06	.59	.26	.07	.98	.05	.62	.23	.09	.99
Special Schools	M	.00	.72	.17	.07	.96	.10	.75	.16	.00	1.00
	F	.12	.73	.05	.09	.99	.07	.80	.09	.03	.99
Junior Colleges[b]	M	.03	.34	.52	.09	.98	.06	.44	.39	.08	.97
	F	.02	.53	.35	.09	.99	.03	.56	.30	.09	.98
Senior Colleges	M	.01	.04	.55	.39	.99	.01	.03	.60	.35	.99
	F	.01	.06	.72	.20	.99	.01	.09	.72	.17	.99
All Students	M	.15	.19	.42	.21	.97	.21	.29	.33	.14	.97
	F	.21	.31	.35	.10	.97	.18	.41	.30	.09	.98

[a]Does not include "don't know" responses.
[b]Defined as two years, less than four years.

not expect to terminate their education there. In both Illinois and California, 58 percent of the SCOPE students who enrolled in junior colleges aspired to a four-year degree or more. This percentage was not much lower in Massachusetts (53 percent) but did drop significantly in North Carolina (43 percent).

As a pattern, girls have lower educational aspirations than do boys. This can easily be discerned by looking at the bottom row, "All Students," of Table 5-8. Girls are slightly more inclined to say that a high school education is enough; they are much more content than boys to settle for "Some College," and then are consistently lower in ambition than boys for a "4-Year Degree" or "Postgraduate Degree." This pattern of sex differences in aspiration is most notable among those students who planned to go to college but did not go. The pattern begins to blur a bit in the group who enrolled in junior colleges and becomes quite scrambled for the group who entered four-year colleges or universities. Even with this last group, however, the aspiration of the boys for postbaccalaureate education far surpassed that of girls. Note also, that among those who entered junior colleges the girls are much more content than the boys to limit their aspirations to "Some College."

Valuable answers will appear whether the research question is asked, "What were the 1966 educational aspiration of the students in the 1967 categories of outcome?" or the obverse question, "What were the categories of outcome for each of the four levels of student aspirations?" The composite percentages given in Table 5-9 were derived as answers to the latter question.

Marked differences by state and by sex will also show up in the

Table 5-9. Postsecondary Outcomes Compared with the Educational Aspirations of SCOPE Seniors

Student Aspiration Levels	Postsecondary Outcomes				
	No College				
	No Plan To Go	Planned To Go	Special Schools	Junior College	Senior College
High School Only	.83				
	.60	.23	.04	.11	.02
Some College	.23	.28	.02	.36	.11
4-Year Graduate	.06	.17	.01	.77	
				.24	.53
Post-Graduate	.05	.15	.01	.77	
				.18	.61

answer either way the research question on student educational aspirations is put. Table 5-10 again keeps educational aspiration as the constant factor and post-secondary outcomes as the variable and then gives a detailed breakdown by state and by sex.

Observe how the accessibility of the junior colleges in California keeps affecting the results. Among California boys and girls who said high school or vocational school was enough, a lower percentage ended up outside college, i.e., more of them changed their minds and enrolled in junior colleges instead. The same state difference applies to the boys and girls who aspired to "Some College." This difference (California vis-à-vis Illinois, Massachusetts, and North Carolina) is even more pronounced among students who aspired to a four-year degree and continues among students who set their sights at more than a four-year degree. The explanation, of course, is that the junior college is seen, particularly in California, as the beginning means toward whatever educational end the students may have in mind. The unique perception of the junior college in California is further demonstrated by the fact that students in Illinois, Massachusetts, and North Carolina who aspired to a four-year degree or more than a four-year degree were much more likely than California students to enter four-year colleges or universities.

As to sex differences, girls are somewhat more likely than boys to limit their educational ambition to high school and then not exceed this ambition. If girls have B.A. degree expectations, they are much more inclined than boys to enter a four-year college or university to fulfill this expectation. This sex difference reverses itself among students who aspire to master's or Ph.D. degrees: within this group there are, in gross numbers, twice as many boys as girls; and, except in California, there is a higher percentage of boys than girls who enter four-year colleges or universities.

An incidental point or two deserve mention while we are on the subject of student educational aspiration compared with what the students actually did. The first point: there is *prima facie* evidence that the more prestigious the institution, the more academically committed the students are who enter it. Practically no one among the SCOPE seniors went to a Ph.D.-granting university who was not committed at least to a baccalaureate if not a graduate degree. On the other hand, 42 percent of the SCOPE seniors who went to junior colleges said, while still seniors, that they did not want to complete a four-year degree. The second point: the discrepancy between 80 percent of the SCOPE seniors aspiring and only 52 percent going to college should not be dismissed as a temporary state of affairs soon to be corrected by delayed entrance. The optimists should be disabused of the assumption that large numbers of students who do not matriculate immediately after high school will do so later. Medsker and Trent [1965a] reported that only four percent of the 10,000 seniors in their study became late entrants into college and even these were plagued by high attrition rates.

Table 5-10. Postsecondary Outcomes Compared with Educational Aspirations of SCOPE Seniors (by State and by Sex)

Students' Educational Aspirations		California						Illinois					
		No College		Spec Schls	Jr Coll[b]	Sr Coll	Total[a]	No College		Spec Schls	Jr Coll[b]	Sr Coll	Total[a]
		No Plan To Go	Did Plan To Go					No Plan To Go	Did Plan To Go				
High School Only	M	.77	.10	.00	.11	.02	1.00	.87	.08	.00	.03	.02	1.00
	F	.81	.08	.02	.07	.01	.99	.93	.04	.01	.02	.01	1.00
Some College	M	.23	.29	.01	.45	.03	1.00	.33	.35	.02	.24	.07	1.00
	F	.18	.32	.07	.37	.06	1.00	.29	.36	.05	.19	.11	1.00
4-Year Graduate	M	.07	.15	.00	.52	.26	1.00	.06	.18	.00	.21	.55	1.00
	F	.02	.14	.00	.36	.47	.99	.05	.14	.01	.16	.65	1.00
Post-Graduate	M	.04	.15	.00	.35	.46	1.00	.03	.12	.00	.19	.67	1.00
	F	.04	.19	.01	.29	.47	1.00	.06	.17	.01	.16	.60	1.00
All Students	M	.22	.17	.00	.40	.20	.99	.26	.19	.00	.18	.37	1.00
	F	.21	.21	.02	.32	.23	.99	.33	.19	.02	.14	.32	1.00

Postsecondary Outcomes

		Massachusetts						North Carolina					
High School Only	M	.86	.05	.00	.02	.02	.95	.83	.09	.01	.04	.02	.99
	F	.91	.04	.02	.02	.01	1.00	.91	.07	.01	.02	.01	1.00
Some College	M	.28	.31	.04	.29	.09	1.00	.34	.37	.03	.23	.03	1.00
	F	.29	.27	.10	.28	.06	1.00	.31	.38	.07	.18	.05	.99
4-Year Graduate	M	.08	.15	.00	.20	.56	.99	.10	.21	.01	.18	.50	1.00
	F	.03	.11	.01	.17	.69	1.00	.05	.20	.01	.13	.61	1.00
Post-Graduate	M	.02	.10	.00	.07	.80	.99	.08	.14	.00	.09	.69	1.00
	F	.07	.09	.04	.15	.65	1.00	.11	.26	.01	.13	.48	.99
All Students	M	.24	.16	.01	.16	.42	.99	.34	.22	.01	.15	.28	1.00
	F	.32	.14	.04	.17	.33	1.00	.33	.25	.04	.13	.25	1.00

[a]Does not include "don't know" responses.
[b]Defined as two years, less than four years.

INTELLECTUAL PREDISPOSITION AND
COLLEGE CHOICE

The Center for Research and Development in Higher Education has long been interested in the attraction that various types of collegiate institutions have for students with diverse measures on noncognitive scales. The Omnibus Personality Inventory (OPI) developed from this interest [Heist and Yonge 1968]. For the specific purpose of securing a measure of intellectual predisposition (IPD), a mini-inventory was incorporated into the SCOPE questionnaire which used the most discriminating items from the Thinking Introversion, Theoretical Orientation and Autonomy scales of the OPI. The general hypothesis was that students with high scores on the IPD scale would demonstrate greater interest in and commitment to the ideational and academic aspects of school life than would those with low scores. The concern within the context of this chapter is the more specific hypothesis that students with different IPD scores would have different outcomes after high school. And, indeed they did, as can be seen easily when the data is presented in the composite form of Table 5-11.

Several significant conclusions can be drawn from Table 5-11 that tend to be hidden by details when the data is broken down by state and by sex. Note first that almost half of the students in the lowest IPD quartile neither planned to go nor went to college, and almost half of the students in the highest IPD quartile ended up in four-year colleges or universities. Second, observe how closely the junior colleges came to drawing students almost equally from all four IPD levels. This is a most descriptive indication of the diverse mix of students in these institutions—some with high intellectual orientation and others who are very practical-minded and relatively unconcerned with abstract ideas and new values. Lastly, note how the students who planned to go to college but did not go resemble the junior college group as opposed to the group

Table 5-11.   Postsecondary Outcomes Compared with Intellectual Predisposition Levels of SCOPE Seniors

Intellectual Predisposition Levels	Postsecondary Outcomes				
	No College				
	No Plan To Go	*Planned To Go*	*Special Schools*	*Junior Colleges*	*Senior Colleges*
Lowest Quartile	.46	.20	.03	.18	.11
3rd Quartile	.33	.22	.02	.21	.21
2nd Quartile	.22	.20	.02	.21	.34
Highest Quartile	.14	.18	.01	.21	.45

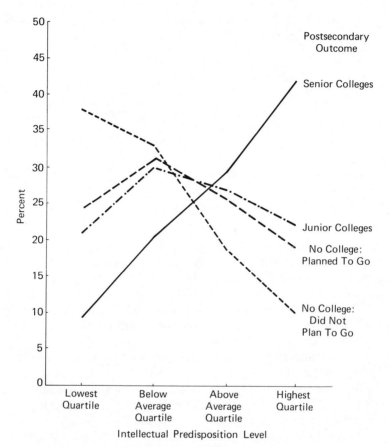

Figure 5-1. Profiles of Intellectual Predisposition Scores for Four Outcome Groups of 1966 SCOPE Seniors

who never planned to go and never went to college. They appear to be the most promising recruitment pool for junior colleges.

Figure 5-1 conveys the differences among four outcome groups: those who did not plan to go to college and did not go, those who planned to go but did not go to college, those who went to junior college, and those who enrolled in senior institutions. On this measure, as in most distributions, the junior college curve is quite normative. Furthermore, it is remarkably similar to that of the subgroup "No College: Planned To Go". The other subgroup, "No College: Did Not Plan To Go," is far from normative but rather is an almost exact reversal of the senior college group.

Intellectual predisposition is really an amalgam of a complex of

Table 5-12.   Distribution of Intellectual Predisposition of SCOPE Seniors (by State)

	Intellectual Predisposition			
State	Lowest Quartile	3rd Quartile	2nd Quartile	Highest Quartile
California	.20	.25	.26	.29
Illinois	.23	.27	.24	.25
Massachusetts	.22	.26	.25	.27
North Carolina	.26	.31	.25	.17

values, and people's values are absorbed from their personal and social environments. At least by stereotype, urban, cosmopolitan states should register higher on statewide IPD measure than more rural and perhaps provincial states. California does tend to the high side on IPD scores and North Carolina to the low, while Illinois and Massachusetts are balanced in between. This can be seen in Table 5-12 which records state precentages by the four IPD categories independent of postsecondary outcome.

What about differences in intellectual predisposition by sex? Male chauvinists would say that men are more intellectually oriented than women, and the Women's Liberation Front would certainly be vociferous in its contradiction. Using the SCOPE sample and the SCOPE instrument, the males have no basis for their chauvinism, a conclusion illustrated in Table 5-13.

So, this inquiry has demonstrated very little difference in IPD by state and even less by sex. However, composite calculations can iron out differences that really exist; hence, it is possible that when parsed out by postsecondary outcome, state and sex difference will appear. Table 5-14 records the comparison, by state and sex, of intellectual predisposition with each of the five categories of postsecondary outcome.

Table 5-13.   Distribution of Intellectual Predisposition of SCOPE Seniors (by Sex)

	Intellectual Predisposition			
Sex	Lowest Quartile	3rd Quartile	2nd Quartile	Highest Quartile
Male	.22	.28	.26	.24
Female	.24	.28	.25	.23

Table 5-14. Intellectual Predisposition of SCOPE Seniors (N = 33,126) Compared with Postsecondary Outcomes (by State and by Sex)

			Intellectual Predisposition									
			California					*Illinois*				
Postsecondary Outcomes			*Low*	*Below Aver*	*Above Aver*	*High*	*Total*	*Low*	*Below Aver*	*Above Aver*	*High*	*Total*
No College	No Plan To Go	M	.37	.31	.20	.16	1.00	.39	.31	.18	.12	1.00
		F	.35	.32	.21	.12	1.00	.40	.33	.17	.10	1.00
	Planned To Go	M	.20	.30	.26	.23	1.00	.23	.33	.24	.21	1.00
		F	.23	.24	.27	.26	1.00	.26	.26	.26	.22	1.00
Special Schools		M	.25	.25	.50	.00	1.00	.29	.38	.24	.10	1.00
		F	.31	.32	.20	.17	1.00	.39	.35	.15	.11	1.00
Junior Colleges[a]		M	.18	.28	.28	.27	1.00	.21	.30	.24	.26	1.00
		F	.20	.25	.26	.20	1.00	.18	.28	.29	.26	1.00
Senior Colleges		M	.05	.13	.28	.54	1.00	.09	.22	.30	.39	1.00
		F	.07	.15	.27	.52	1.00	.09	.20	.28	.43	1.00
All Students		M	.19	.26	.26	.29	1.00	.22	.28	.25	.26	1.00
		F	.22	.25	.26	.28	1.00	.24	.27	.24	.25	1.00

Table 5-14. Continued

		Intellectual Predisposition									
		Massachusetts					North Carolina				
Postsecondary Outcomes		Low	Below Aver	Above Aver	High	Total	Low	Below Aver	Above Aver	High	Total
No College	No Plan To Go										
	M	.35	.29	.23	.13	1.00	.37	.34	.20	.08	1.00
	F	.41	.29	.18	.12	1.00	.38	.35	.19	.07	1.00
	Planned To Go										
	M	.20	.34	.26	.19	1.00	.26	.34	.28	.12	1.00
	F	.29	.28	.22	.21	1.00	.25	.34	.27	.15	1.00
Special Schools	M	.28	.24	.38	.10	1.00	.40	.25	.25	.10	1.00
	F	.27	.32	.28	.13	1.00	.33	.36	.22	.08	1.00
Junior Colleges[a]	M	.19	.36	.29	.16	1.00	.29	.34	.22	.15	1.00
	F	.20	.29	.29	.23	1.00	.24	.35	.29	.12	1.00
Senior Colleges	M	.09	.18	.30	.43	1.00	.10	.21	.32	.37	1.00
	F	.09	.18	.25	.48	1.00	.13	.24	.30	.33	1.00
All Students	M	.19	.26	.27	.27	1.00	.26	.30	.25	.18	1.00
	F	.24	.25	.23	.27	1.00	.26	.32	.25	.16	1.00

[a]Defined as two years, less than four years.

Although there are minor differences by sex, no discernable pattern pops out of Table 5-14. There are some side IPD differences by sex within the "Special Schools" outcome, but very few of the 1966 SCOPE graduates enrolled in such special schools.

There are several differences among states, particularly between California and North Carolina as presaged by the data assembled in Table 5-12. California was markedly higher than North Carolina in the "Highest IPD" column no matter whether it was for the "No Plan To Go" outcome or the "Senior Colleges" outcome. North Carolina had higher percentages of students with low IPD in the junior colleges than did California or, for that matter, than either of the other two states. California had significantly higher percentages even than Massachusetts of SCOPE seniors matriculating to senior colleges who had IPD scores ranked in the highest quartile.

Quite apart from the data on intellectual predisposition presented here, there is clear evidence from the SCOPE Project that the institutions which attracted the most intellectually disposed students were the independent universities. Over 60 percent of these seniors were in the top quartile on the IPD scale and only 5 percent in the bottom quartile. In contrast, over one-third of the students who went to independent vocational schools were in the lowest quartile and only 10 percent in the highest.

The SCOPE Project was, as noted earlier, a five-year longitudinal study; therefore, more is to be reported in subsequent publications on the constancy of IPD measure over time, on the relationship of IPD to family background, on the congruence with academic aptitudes, and on several other related matters. The focus of this report will now shift to socioeconomic status and its relationship to the way in which students distributed themselves among the categories of postsecondary outcomes.

Chapter Six

Socioeconomic Factors

Everyone seems to know what social class is until they begin to define it. The first line to which semantic retreat is made is the phrase socioeconomic status. This term sounds disarmingly innocuous and is, perhaps, more amenable to measurement. However, the problems do not end here. A further difficulty in educational research is that young people do not have a socioeconomic status independent of their parents and, if asked, will not be able to give a categorical and reliable estimate of parental socioeconomic status (SES). So further retreat is made to straightforward questions on such variables as occupational level of father and/or educational level of parents and/or family income and/or any number of other factors from which socioeconomic status can be inferred. Within the entire longitudinal SCOPE Project, most conceivable measures of SES were eventually ascertained. However, for the purpose of this distribution study of the first cohort of SCOPE seniors, inference of SES was limited to occupational level of father and to family income.

OCCUPATIONAL LEVEL OF FATHERS AND POSTSECONDARY OUTCOMES

The relationship between education and occupation in America has long been a central issue in social research. The stereotype about this relationship "has been that professional men have been to college, other white collar people have been to high school, while manual workers, by and large, have not gone beyond grade school" [Trow 1967, p. 25]. As late as 1950, this stereotype was largely confirmed by data from the U.S. Census. Using this data, Bogue [1959] calculated the median years of schooling completed by men and women twenty-five years of age or older, as shown in Table 6-1.

However, awesome changes occurred between 1950 and 1966. The remarkable increase in college-going since World War II, as shown in Figure 6-1,

Table 6-1.   Median Years of Education for Various Occupational
Levels (1950)

Occupational Levels	Years of Education
Professionals	16 +
Managers, Officers, Proprietors	11.3
Clerical and Kindred	11.4
Sales Workers	11.2
Craftsmen, Foremen and Kindred	8.3
Operators and Kindred	7.7
Laborers, except Mine and Farm	7.0
Service Workers	7.8

Source: Bogue, 1959.

invites inquiry on changes that have taken place in the relationship between education and socioeconomic status.

The upward curve of college enrollment is not as egalitarian as it might appear. Much of this rise in college attendance has resulted from increasing proportions of students from families of middle- to high-occupational status entering college rather than from significant progress in closing the educational gap between the high- and low-occupational strata of American society. In 1959, Medsker and Trent found that the percentage of families who sent their children to college dropped steadily with the descending level of father's occupation. Their findings, summarized in Table 6-2, led them to conclude that college attendance was more closely related to father's occupation than to the student's ability level [Medsker and Trent 1965a].

The decade of the 1960s was devoted largely to removing barriers to admission to college, and thus it was oriented toward gaining access for groups that had never before considered attending college. Emphasis upon access assumes that the task is to change students to fit the system; emphasis upon accommodation implies that the system can be changed to fit the students. Both access and accom-

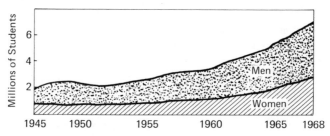

Figure 6-1.   Opening Fall Enrollments of All Students in All Institutions by Sex (1946-1968) *Source:* American Council on Education, 1969.

Table 6-2. Percentage of High School Graduates Attending College in 1959 by Levels of Father's Occupation

Father's Occupation	Percent of Graduates Entering College
Professional I (High)	.78
Professional II (Low)	.73
Managers–Executives	.72
Small Business Owners	.55
Sales and Clerical	.52
Skilled Workers	.37
Semi- and Unskilled Workers	.28

Source: Medsker and Trent, 1965a.

modation are designed to narrow the gap between educational opportunities and students; access predominated in the '60s and accommodation must receive the major attention of the '70s. [Cross 1971, p. 70]

Cross goes on to describe the increasing severity of the selection process as students advance in the system. "For every 100 students entering the fifth grade, approximately 72 graduate from high school, 40 enter college, 20 graduate from college, 5 obtain master's degrees, and roughly one in a hundred citizens who were fifth graders in 1960 may expect to receive the doctor's degree" [Cross 1971, p. 74].

The 1966 SCOPE data, summarized in Table 6-3, would suggest encouraging but modest increases in participation in postsecondary education by the children from families of middle- and low-level occupations. It is important to note, however, that neither the classification system nor the samples for these two studies are the same. Even though both studies used large representative samples of students, only the trends can be viewed with confidence.

The relationship between occupational level of family and outcome after high school is graphically displayed in Figure 6-2, in which the percentages of senior college, junior college, and noncollege groups are plotted for each family occupational level.

The SCOPE data presented thus far has been in composite form simply to show trends. It leaves unanswered questions of differences by state and by sex. This will now be done first by asking the research question, "What were the fathers' occupational levels (SES) of the 1966 SCOPE seniors for each of the 1967 categories of postsecondary outcome?" and then reversing the question to "What were the categories of postsecondary outcome for the children falling within each of the three levels of fathers' occupations?"

Table 6-4 zeroes in on state differences and clearly reveals California as the exception. The fathers of 40 percent of the California SCOPE seniors were classified at the managerial and professional level (III), and only 21 percent

Table 6-3. Percentage of 1966 SCOPE Seniors Attending College from Homes of Differing Occupational Levels

Father's Occupation	*Percent of SCOPE Seniors in College*
Very High Level	
Professional (High)	.82
Elected Officials	.72
Managers–Executives	.71
Professional (Low)	.70
High Level	
Artists and Entertainers	.63
Salesmen	.63
Business Owners	.61
Technicians	.60
Office Workers	.60
Moderate Level	
Skilled Craftsmen	.46
Farm Owner	.46
Service Worker	.45
Low Level	
Machine Operator	.35
Workman	.33

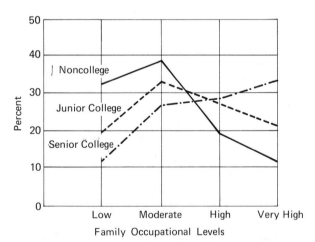

Figure 6-2. Percentage of 1966 SCOPE Seniors Who Went to Senior College, Junior College, and Who Did Not Go to College for Each of Four Family Occupational Levels

Table 6–4. Fathers' Occupational Levels (SES) of SCOPE Seniors (N = 31,544) with Different Postsecondary Outcomes (by State)

Postsecondary Outcomes		California Blue Collar & Serv	California White Collar & Skld	California Mana-gerial & Prof	California Total	Illinois Blue Collar & Serv	Illinois White Collar & Skld	Illinois Mana-gerial & Prof	Illinois Total
No College	No Plan To Go	.32	.42	.27	1.00	.44	.36	.20	1.00
	Planned To Go	.26	.39	.35	1.00	.35	.41	.24	1.00
Special Schools		.32	.45	.24	1.00	.37	.35	.28	1.00
Junior College[a]		.20	.40	.40	1.00	.32	.38	.30	1.00
Senior College		.09	.30	.60	1.00	.16	.43	.41	1.00
All Students		.21	.36	.40	1.00	.29	.40	.30	1.00

Postsecondary Outcomes		Massachusetts Blue Collar & Serv	Massachusetts White Collar & Skld	Massachusetts Mana-gerial & Prof	Massachusetts Total	North Carolina Blue Collar & Serv	North Carolina White Collar & Skld	North Carolina Mana-gerial & Prof	North Carolina Total
No College	No Plan To Go	.45	.39	.16	1.00	.47	.32	.20	1.00
	Planned To Go	.33	.38	.29	1.00	.44	.32	.24	1.00
Special Schools		.37	.39	.24	1.00	.42	.34	.24	1.00
Junior College[a]		.34	.39	.27	1.00	.26	.41	.33	1.00
Senior College		.22	.35	.44	1.00	.19	.39	.42	1.00
All Students		.32	.37	.31	1.00	.36	.35	.29	1.00

Fathers' Occupation

[a] Defined as two years, less than four years.

Table 6-5. Fathers' Occupational Level (SES) of SCOPE Seniors with Different Postsecondary Outcomes (by State and by Sex)

Postsecondary Outcomes		Fathers' Occupation							
		California				Illinois			
		Blue Collar & Serv	White Collar & Skld	Managerial & Prof	Total	Blue Collar & Serv	White Collar & Skld	Managerial & Prof	Total
No College — No Plan To Go	M	.32	.42	.27	1.00	.43	.37	.21	1.00
	F	.32	.42	.27	1.00	.44	.36	.20	1.00
No College — Planned To Go	M	.26	.39	.36	1.00	.35	.41	.25	1.00
	F	.26	.40	.34	1.00	.34	.42	.24	1.00
Special Schools	M	.67	.33	.00	1.00	.40	.35	.25	1.00
	F	.31	.45	.24	1.00	.37	.35	.28	1.00
Junior College[a]	M	.22	.39	.39	1.00	.36	.36	.28	1.00
	F	.18	.40	.42	1.00	.27	.41	.32	1.00
Senior College	M	.12	.30	.59	1.00	.18	.34	.47	1.00
	F	.07	.31	.61	1.00	.13	.46	.37	1.00
All Students	M	.23	.38	.40	1.00	.31	.36	.33	1.00
	F	.20	.38	.41	1.00	.28	.43	.29	1.00

		Massachusetts				*North Carolina*			
No College	No Plan To Go	M	.44	.38	.18	1.00	.47	.33	.20	1.00
		F	.46	.40	.14	1.00	.48	.32	.20	1.00
	Planned To Go	M	.32	.39	.29	1.00	.42	.34	.24	1.00
		F	.33	.38	.29	1.00	.46	.31	.24	1.00
Special Schools		M	.37	.52	.11	1.00	.54	.20	.26	1.00
		F	.37	.36	.26	1.00	.39	.38	.24	1.00
Junior College[a]		M	.36	.42	.23	1.00	.27	.42	.32	1.00
		F	.31	.37	.32	1.00	.26	.40	.34	1.00
Senior College		M	.22	.37	.41	1.00	.18	.39	.43	1.00
		F	.21	.31	.47	1.00	.21	.39	.40	1.00
All Students		M	.31	.38	.31	1.00	.35	.36	.29	1.00
		F	.33	.36	.31	1.00	.37	.35	.28	1.00

[a]Defined as two years, less than four years.

were classified at the blue collar and service occupations level (I). The high for
SES level III is nine percentage points above the next highest state, Massachusetts,
and the low for SES I is eight percentage points below the next lowest state,
Illinois. This statewide difference held consistently at every category of postsecondary outcome. Among the SCOPE seniors who neither planned nor went
to college, California had a higher percentage whose fathers were managerial and
professional and a lower percentage whose fathers were in blue collar and
service occupations. Again, among the SCOPE seniors who enrolled in either
junior colleges or in senior colleges, California had the highest percentage whose
fathers were managerial and professional and the lowest percentage whose
fathers were blue collar or service workers. In all instances, these percentage
differences between California and the other three states were wide enough to
be significant at least at the .05 level of confidence.

The 1966 data on major occupational groups for American males
from the Bureau of the Census gives some base point for understanding these
state differences just reported. By reclassifying this data to coincide with the
SCOPE classifications, American males in 1966 were distributed as follows across
the three occupational groups [U.S. Department of Commerce 1967]:

Blue collar and service	36%
White collar and skilled	35%
Managerial and professional	25%

In all four states, those who planned to go to college but did not go
registered a higher SES level than those who never planned to go to college and
who, in fact, did not go. Actually, the distribution by SES level for the "planned/
no go" groups looked more like the distribution for the "junior college" groups
than like the distribution of the "no plan/no go" groups. In turn, the distribution
of the "junior college" groups seemed to fall in the middle ground between the
"no college" and the "senior college" groups. It is remarkable how evenly the
children from SES II, white collar and skilled, distribute themselves over the five
categories of postsecondary outcome.

Since there were some basic sex differences in regard to the postsecondary outcomes of SCOPE seniors, it was anticipated that SES would be one
of the contributing factors. This does not seem to be the case. The rarity of
sex differences by SES (fathers' occupational levels) is, in itself, noteworthy.
Table 6-5 demonstrates this point.

Disregarding the special schools outcome (where the small numbers
make large differences of doubtful significance), there are very few instances of
notable sex differences. Among entering students in Illinois junior colleges, the
sons of blue collar fathers are more highly represented than are their daughters;
and, to lesser degrees, this is also true in the other three states. In all four states
the percentage of junior college girls from SES III, managerial and professional,

Table 6-6. Postsecondary Outcomes of SCOPE Seniors from Families in High, Middle, and Low Levels of Socioeconomic Status (by State)

Postsecondary Outcomes

California

Fathers' Occupation	No College		Spec Schls	Jr Coll[a]	Sr Coll	Total
	No Plan To Go	Did Plan To Go				
Blue Collar & Service	.30	.23	.02	.35	.10	1.00
White Collar & Skilled	.22	.19	.02	.38	.18	1.00
Managerial & Professional	.13	.16	.01	.36	.33	1.00
All Students	.20	.19	.02	.37	.23	1.00

Massachusetts

Fathers' Occupation	No College		Spec Schls	Jr Coll[a]	Sr Coll	Total
	No Plan To Go	Did Plan To Go				
Blue Collar & Service	.38	.15	.03	.17	.27	1.00
White Collar & Skilled	.28	.15	.03	.17	.36	1.00
Managerial & Professional	.14	.14	.02	.15	.55	1.00
All Students	.27	.15	.03	.17	.39	1.00

Illinois

Fathers' Occupation	No College		Spec Schls	Jr Coll[a]	Sr Coll	Total
	No Plan To Go	Did Plan To Go				
Blue Collar & Service	.41	.21	.02	.17	.20	1.00
White Collar & Skilled	.25	.18	.01	.15	.41	1.00
Managerial & Professional	.18	.14	.01	.15	.52	1.00
All Students	.28	.18	.01	.15	.38	1.00

North Carolina

Fathers' Occupation	No College		Spec Schls	Jr Coll[a]	Sr Coll	Total
	No Plan To Go	Did Plan To Go				
Blue Collar & Service	.43	.29	.03	.11	.15	1.00
White Collar & Skilled	.30	.21	.02	.17	.30	1.00
Managerial & Professional	.23	.19	.02	.17	.39	1.00
All Students	.33	.23	.02	.14	.27	1.00

[a]Defined as two years, less than four years.

Table 6-7. Family Income (SES) of SCOPE Seniors (N = 33,094) with Different Postsecondary Outcomes (by State)

	Family Income											
	California						*Illinois*					
Postsecondary Outcomes	*Much Higher Than Aver*	*Higher Than Aver*	*Aver*	*Lower Than Aver*	*Much Lower Than Aver*	*Total[a]*	*Much Higher Than Aver*	*Higher Than Aver*	*Aver*	*Lower Than Aver*	*Much Lower Than Aver*	*Total[a]*
No College — No Plan To Go	.11	.27	.26	.10	.04	.78	.07	.23	.31	.13	.04	.80
No College — Planned To Go	.13	.32	.27	.10	.04	.86	.12	.33	.28	.10	.02	.85
Special Schools	.09	.25	.31	.12	.07	.84	.06	.27	.31	.15	.02	.81
Junior Colleges[b]	.16	.40	.23	.07	.03	.89	.11	.36	.29	.09	.02	.87
Senior Colleges	.29	.43	.15	.05	.01	.93	.21	.41	.20	.05	.02	.89
All Students	.17	.36	.23	.08	.03	.87	.13	.33	.27	.09	.03	.85

		Massachusetts						North Carolina				
No College	No Plan To Go	.05	.18	.31	.12	.04	.70	.03	.11	.34	.21	.10	.79
	Planned To Go	.11	.25	.29	.08	.03	.76	.05	.16	.26	.21	.11	.79
Special Schools		.04	.22	.31	.07	.03	.67	.03	.17	.40	.18	.05	.83
Junior Colleges[b]		.09	.30	.31	.10	.02	.82	.09	.25	.30	.16	.05	.85
Senior Colleges		.17	.39	.23	.08	.03	.90	.13	.32	.25	.13	.07	.90
All Students		.11	.29	.28	.09	.03	.80	.07	.20	.28	.18	.09	.82

[a]Does not include "don't know" responses.
[b]Defined as two years, less than four years.

is higher than the percentage of boys from this SES level. Even when sex differences do appear, they are often inconsistent and seem to have no pattern. In the "senior college" outcome the message is very mixed: a slightly higher percentage of boys than girls from SES III is found in Illinois and North Carolina while a reversal of this is true of California and Massachusetts. The overall conclusion to be drawn from the data in Table 6-5 is that sex differences in postsecondary outcomes will have to be explained on bases other than the socioeconomic status of family.

When the research question concerning SES is reversed it reads, "How fared the children coming from each of the three levels of socioeconomic status?" The answer, to be found in Table 6-6, will confirm the obvious but will, at the same time, reveal that the obvious is relative, requires qualification, and is being eroded by change.

Youngsters whose fathers are in managerial and professional occupations are more likely to enroll in senior colleges than youngsters whose fathers are in blue collar and service occupations. But, this was not true of those enrolling in junior colleges. The claim that junior colleges are institutions that foster the democratization of higher education is born out by the facts. In all states, the junior colleges drew almost equally from the three socioeconomic levels, yet note the differences in percentages between California and the other three states. California had 60 percent of its sample entering college, yet the percentage of students from the low, the middle, and the high SES groups who enroll in California senior colleges was much lower than for the other three states. Why? Because the percentage from each SES group entering the community colleges was twice again as high in California as any other state.

Actually, Table 6-6 is heartening for those who like to think that the education system does contribute to social mobility in the United States. North Carolina had 26 percent of students from blue collar families entering some degree-granting college—and North Carolina was fourth in this regard: Illinois had 37 percent, Massachusetts had 44 percent, and California had 45 percent of youngsters from SES I entering college. Of course, there is the pessimistic reversal of this observation: in North Carolina 72 percent, in Illinois 62 percent, and in Massachusetts and California 53 percent of the sons and daughters of blue collar workers ended their formal education at the twelfth grade.

The SCOPE seniors from white collar families, being middle-middle class, distribute themselves by "outcome" as if, by predetermination, they constituted the mean. In each state, the percentage figures in the "White Collar" row looks like a replication of the percentage figures in the "All Students" row. This does not necessarily mean that this group is stymied at dead center. Far from it! In all states many are securing the education that could elevate them from SES II to SES III.

FAMILY INCOME AND POSTSECONDARY
OUTCOMES

The other measure of socioeconomic status (SES) used in this first distribution study of the SCOPE Project was that of family income. Each SCOPE senior was asked to rate the income of his family against the 1966 average income of $6,200 on the 5-point scale of (1) much higher, (2) higher, (3) average, (4) lower, and (5) much lower. This data on family income is presented in Table 6-7 as percentages falling within each postsecondary outcome.

One fact that is striking from even a casual glance at Table 27 is that North Carolina is the only state of the four in which affluence approximates a normal curve. In the other three states, only 11 or 12 percent of the students rate their family incomes as below average. It does not appear that disproportionate percentages of students rate their family income as "much higher than average"; rather, SCOPE seniors simply are, or think they are, middle class.

Family income is, of course, another measure of socioeconomic status, hence it should be no surprise that students in four-year colleges and universities tend to come from families with higher or much higher-than-average incomes. Since the distribution by outcome is skewed to average or above, it is not surprising to find that even students who did not go on to college are also more likely to come from families who are above average in income than from families below average in income. The one exception is North Carolina, the only state in which family income followed a normal curve.

Some other observations are worthy of note:

1. The distribution of family income of students enrolled in junior colleges in each state is almost indistinguishable from the distribution of family income of all students in that state.
2. Although many students from families with above-average income do not go to college, not many students from families with below-average income enroll in senior colleges or in junior colleges.
3. Those students claiming average family income distributed themselves rather evenly over all postsecondary outcomes except senior college. Put more sharply, modest family income is significantly less of a barrier to enrollment in junior colleges than to enrollment in senior colleges.
4. The percentage of junior college students reporting higher-than-average family income is significantly less than for senior college students, but the dramatic separation between these two outcomes occurs (except in North Carolina) among students reporting much higher-than-average family income.
5. Family income is less a determinant of enrollment in senior colleges in North Carolina than it is in the other states.

Table 6-8.   Postsecondary Outcomes of SCOPE Seniors with Different Family Income Levels (SES) (by State)

	Postsecondary Outcomes											
	California						Illinois					
	No College		Spec Schls	Jr Coll[a]	Sr Coll	Total	No College		Spec Schls	Jr Coll[a]	Sr Coll	Total
Family Income	No Plan To Go	Did Plan To Go					No Plan To Go	Did Plan To Go				
Much Higher Than Average	.14	.15	.01	.34	.37	1.00	.16	.17	.01	.12	.55	1.00
Higher Than Average	.16	.17	.01	.40	.26	1.00	.21	.19	.01	.17	.43	1.00
Average	.24	.24	.02	.36	.15	1.00	.35	.20	.01	.18	.26	1.00
Lower Than Average	.28	.25	.03	.31	.14	1.00	.43	.21	.02	.15	.19	1.00
Much Lower Than Average	.28	.24	.04	.35	.10	1.00	.42	.17	.01	.13	.27	1.00
All Students	.21	.19	.02	.36	.22	1.00	.30	.19	.01	.16	.34	1.00

	Massachusetts						North Carolina					
Much Higher Than Average	.12	.15	.01	.13	.59	1.00	.18	.18	.01	.17	.47	1.00
Higher Than Average	.18	.13	.02	.17	.51	1.00	.19	.19	.02	.18	.42	1.00
Average	.32	.16	.03	.19	.30	1.00	.36	.22	.03	.15	.23	1.00
Lower Than Average	.35	.13	.02	.18	.32	1.00	.39	.27	.02	.13	.19	1.00
Much Lower Than Average	.35	.15	.02	.09	.39	1.00	.37	.31	.02	.08	.22	1.00
All Students	.28	.15	.03	.16	.38	1.00	.34	.24	.02	.14	.26	1.00

aDefined as two years, less than four years.

When the research question is reversed to ask what happened to the students from each of the SES levels as measured by family income, some surprising answers are forthcoming. Look now at Table 6–8. California has very low student representation in senior colleges from families whose incomes are average (15 percent), lower than average (14 percent), or much lower than average (10 percent). Massachusetts, on the other hand, has high student representation in senior colleges from these lower family income levels. Apparently, the open-door, no-tuition community colleges in California serve to let the senior colleges off the hook by allowing them to be less concerned about providing for the low SES student. In California, where 36 percent of the sample enrolled in junior colleges, 35 percent of those with much lower-than-average family income also enrolled in junior colleges. Compare this with 13 percent from this lowest SES level in Illinois and with 9 percent in Massachusetts and 8 percent in North Carolina.

Table 6–8 also demonstrates that, other than in California, those students at family income levels of average or below average are much more likely to have no plans to go to college and, indeed, not go than to plan to go to college but then not go.

SOCIOECONOMIC STATUS AND TYPE OF COLLEGIATE INSTITUTION

It has been documented that children from homes with higher SES are much more likely to go to some college and are more likely to go to four-year colleges and universities than children from homes with average or below-average SES. The junior college movement, particularly in California, has begun to obscure these class lines, yet the generalization still holds. But then the question arises as to qualitative differences in the educational opportunities for the sons and daughters of various SES levels. As higher education becomes more universal and more democratic, does entry into the high prestige institutions become more exclusive and elitist? Indeed, should students be channeled off into institutions of "best fit"? These questions are being asked in greater depth in the longitudinal aspects of SCOPE, but some beginning answers come through in this initial distribution study. For example, 52 percent of the college-goers from high professional families went to private colleges and universities in contrast to 31 percent of the children whose fathers were skilled craftsmen.

There is, of course, great diversity of private institutions, and some have the tradition of accommodating students of both modest abilities and family resources. A better clue is provided by Table 6–9, which shows the selectivity by SES operating in Ph.D.-granting universities. Recalling that 82 percent of children from high professional homes went to college, note now that 43 percent of these students chose universities which offer doctoral degrees. This proportion is in greatest contrast with the rare selection of such universities

Table 6-9. Percentage of 1966 SCOPE College-Goers from Homes
of Differing Occupational Levels Who Went to
Ph.D.-Granting Universities

Father's Occupation	Percent of College-Goers
Professional (High)	43
Office Workers	36
Managers–Executives	35
Elected Officials	34
Artists and Entertainers	28
Professional (Low)	28
Salesmen	25
Business Owners	25
Technicians	22
Farm Owners	20
Skilled Craftsmen	19
Service Workers	18
Workmen	15
Machine Operators	15

by college-goers from the homes of workmen and machine operators. The
general rank order of these fifteen occupational groups is nearly identical to that
of Table 6-3, "Percentage of 1966 SCOPE Seniors Attending College From
Homes of Differing Occupational Levels." There is a noteworthy reversal of
positions of office workers and low professionals–the former ranking second
only to high professionals. Since SCOPE students came generally from young
families, the explanation may be that a number of fathers whose occupations
were listed as office worker are actually moving into junior executive positions
and, typical of this group, are encouraging high educational aspirations for their
children.

Table 6-10. Comparison of Enrollments in Public and Independent
Ph.D.-Granting Universities by Selected Family Income Levels
(N = 3,596)

	Family Income Level		
Ph.D.-Granting University	Total (All Levels Combined)	Much Higher Than Average	Much Lower Than Average
Public	.78	.74	.78
Independent	.22	.26	.22
Total	1.00	1.00	1.00

Another way of testing the influence of SES on selection of institution is to compare family income with the type of college or university attended (see Table 6–10). This was done with the SCOPE college-goers but was limited to the 3,596 students who enrolled in Ph.D.-granting universities. The hypothesis was that those from high SES would be attracted to the independent (private, nondenominational) universities, and students from low SES families would go to the public universities. The data gives only small support to the hypothesis. True, among students going to public universities, 22 percent were from homes with much higher-than-average family income while at independent universities, 28 percent of the students came from this highest SES level. The difference of six percentage points with relatively small numbers is not too impressive. There was a marked sex difference in enrollment in independent versus public universities, with the percentages for males climbing from 58 percent public to 64 percent independent and the female percentages making a reciprocal drop from 42 percent public to 36 percent independent. However, this sex difference seemed unrelated to family income. Further, the across-the-board separation was 78 percent public and 22 percent independent, while the division among students from homes with much higher-than-average family income was 74 percent public and 26 percent independent and the division of students from homes with much lower-than-average family income was 78 percent public and 22 percent independent.

This chapter has focused on the evidence relating postsecondary outcome of SCOPE seniors to the socioeconomic status from which they came. SES was certainly demonstrated to be an influential variable, even though the weight of its influence was not always heavy. Although less related than the historical duo of caste and class, another societal determinant that deserves attention next is that of race.

Chapter Seven

Race and Educational Opportunity

In 1966, when the SCOPE questionnaire was given to the first wave of high school seniors, prevailing mores, if not the law, dictated against students classifying themselves by race. The success of the civil rights movement had changed this convention by 1967. Data on race, however, was not secured for the 1966 seniors even though it was obtained on the college-goers among this group when they were canvassed at the end of their freshman year in 1967.[1] This absence of racial data for the 1966 seniors does not nullify other racial data collected, but it does make any argument regarding race as a determinant more circuitous and any conclusions more tenuous. It will require some reliance on comparable information collected in the SCOPE Project on 1969 seniors and will oblige the reader to pay critical attention to how the pieces are put together into a meaningful whole.

BACKGROUND INFORMATION ON RACE

In 1967, the U.S. Department of Commerce estimated that 87.8 percent of Americans were white and 11.2 percent were black [U.S. Department of Commerce 1968]. This differs markedly by age group (the mean ages for blacks and whites are 21 and 28, respectively) and, of course, differs by state. It is germane to this study to note the racial composition of the four sample states, at least the racial mix as recorded in the 1960 Census (see Table 7-1).

1. Usable questionnaires returned by the college students numbered 10,586. Although there was some loss of "lower half" students in reference to ability and family background, the distributions of students from the two samples (all 1966 college-goers and respondents to 1966–67 college questionnaire) were almost identical across institutional types of control. On the other hand, there was a 3 percent underrepresentation of respondents from the two-year institutions.

Table 7-1.   Racial Composition by Number and Percentage of the Four Sample States

State	*White*		*Black*		*Other*	
	Number	*Percent*	*Number*	*Percent*	*Number*	*Percent*
California	14,455,230	91.9	883,861	5.6	378,113	2.4
Illinois	9,010,252	89.4	1,037,470	10.3	33,436	.3
Massachusetts	5,023,144	97.6	111,842	2.2	13,592	.3
North Carolina	3,399,285	74.6	1,116,021	24.5	40,849	.9

Source: U.S. Department of Commerce, 1960.

Table 7-2. Percentage Distribution of 1969 SCOPE Seniors by Race and State (N = 27,112)

State	Caucasian	Negro	American Indian	Oriental/ Asiatic	Mexican-American/ Spanish-American	Mixed/Other
California	.73	.04	.02	.04	.07	.08
Illinois	.78	.07	.03	.02	.01	.08
Massachusetts	.77	.03	.04	.02	.01	.13
North Carolina	.63	.23	.06	.02	.02	.04
Four-State Composite	.73	.11	.04	.02	.02	.07

Table 7-3. Comparison of Racial Distributions of 1969 SCOPE Seniors and 1966–67 SCOPE College Freshmen[a]

SCOPE Samples	Caucasian	Negro	American Indian	Oriental/ Asiatic	Mexican- American/ Spanish- American	Mixed/Other
1969 SCOPE Senior Four-State Composite	.73	.11	.04	.02	.02	.07
1966 SCOPE College Freshmen: Public Institutions Only	.87	.07	.02	.02	.02	--
1966 SCOPE College Freshmen: Public and Private Institutions	.90	.04	.03	.01	.01	--

[a]Does not include "don't know" responses.

RACIAL DISTRIBUTION AT FIRST BRANCHING

As previously explained, it is not known how the 1966 SCOPE seniors were distributed by race. However, it seems reasonable to assume that it would not have differed greatly from the 1969 SCOPE sample of seniors. Figures are available on this group and are presented in Table 7-2 using a more discriminating racial breakdown.

Assume for a moment that the racial mix of the 1966 SCOPE seniors was essentially the same as the 1969 SCOPE seniors, and forget for a moment any success the civil rights movements may have had between 1966 and 1969 in enrolling students from minority backgrounds. If race were not a determinant in college-going, then the racial breakdown of 1966–67 SCOPE college freshmen would approximate the racial composition of the 1969 SCOPE seniors. But that is not the case. The percentage of Caucasians goes up, and the percentage of all other racial groups goes down. This can be seen in Table 7-3 in which the four-state composite of 1969 SCOPE seniors is compared with the four-state composite of 1966–67 SCOPE college freshmen, first by public institutions only and then by combined public and private institutions.

RACIAL DISTRIBUTION WITHIN VARYING
TYPES OF COLLEGIATE INSTITUTIONS

So, at the crucial branching between college and noncollege, the stream of young people going on to college gets whiter. This is not quite so true of enrollments in public institutions, but, due to the long history of segregation of black and American Indian students, these two groups had the highest percentage enrollments in non-public institutions in 1966–67 (see Table 7-4).

Not only does the stream become whiter at the college/noncollege fork, but it becomes progressively whiter by degree-level and prestige of the institution. Although the four-year Negro colleges of North Carolina obscure this trend somewhat, the fact remains that the more select the college, the whiter it is. The Caucasians will capture three-fourths of the seats in any college (except colleges created for blacks and American Indians), but will constitute above 90 percent of the enrollment in M.A.- and Ph.D.-granting institutions (see Table 7-5).

Table 7-5 should also be examined in relationship to Table 7-3. The latter showed that 73 percent of the 1969 SCOPE seniors were Caucasian or, put the other way, 27 percent of these high school graduates were from non-white racial backgrounds. If the 1967 SCOPE seniors approximated this same racial pattern, which is a reasonable assumption, then Table 7-5 carries this disturbing message: the only level of racial equity is that of "less than 2 years of college." The ratios between white and nonwhite extrapolated from Table 7-5 are as follows:

Table 7-4.   Enrollment of 1966-67 SCOPE College Freshmen in Public and Non-public Institutions by Race

Type of Control	Caucasian	Negro	American Indian	Oriental	Mexican- American/ Spanish- American
Public Institution	.62	.56	.58	.83	.69
Non-public Institution	.38	.44	.42	.17	.31
Total	1.00	1.00	1.00	1.00	1.00

Table 7-5. Enrollment of 1966-67 SCOPE College Freshmen by Degree Level of Institution and by Race (N = 9,735)

Race	Less than 2 Years	2 Years, less than 4 Years	4 Years B.A.	More than 4 Years M.A.	More than 4 Years Ph.D.
Caucasian	.75	.87	.88	.93	.94
Negro	.11	.04	.08	.03	.03
American Indian	.09	.04	.03	.02	.01
Oriental	.01	.02	.004	.01	.01
Mexican-American/ Spanish-American	.04	.03	.006	.01	.01
Total	1.00	1.00	1.00	1.00	1.00

Level of Collegiate Institution	*White*	:	*Nonwhite*
Less than 2 years	.75	:	.25
2 years, less than 4 years	.87	:	.13
4 years, B.A.	.88	:	.12
More than 4 years, M.A.	.93	:	.07
More than 4 years, Ph.D.	.94	:	.06

When specific attention is given to the racial characteristics of students who enter the public community colleges, the findings of the SCOPE Project are similar to those of other available studies. This is shown in Table 7-6 after necessary minor adjustments have been made to bring about comparability of distributions.

It is instructive and somewhat heartening to look at the two variables (degree level of institution and race) going the other way. The evidence adds some validity to the conclusions of Patricia Cross [1969] and J. Froomkin [1969] that community colleges are serving and will increasingly serve students from racial and ethnic minorities.

Table 7-7 does show that of those students with colored skins who enter college, a good percentage go to junior colleges. However, the 30 percent figure for black students does not suggest that this racial group is flooding in through the "open doors." Perhaps there was some influx of balck students into public community colleges after 1967; the Department of Health, Education and Welfare figures for 1970 full-time enrollments do show a 1 percent increase over 1967 SCOPE percentages for California and Illinois, though the percentage

Table 7-6.   Enrollments in Public Junior Colleges by Race

Race	SCOPE 1966[d]	BIR[a] 1966[e]	Creager[b] 1968[f]	CGP[c] 1968[g]
Caucasian	.84	.90	.84	.84
Negro	.08	.06	.09	.08
Oriental	.02	.03	.02	.03
Other	.06	.01	.05	(.05)
Total	1.00	1.00	1.00	1.00

[a]From the Bureau of Intergroup Relations, Sacramento, California, State Department of Education, 1966.

[b]Creager et al., 1969.

[c]Cross, 1969.

[d]Eleven percent identified themselves as mixtures of racial/ethnic groups or chose not to respond. The data was adjusted by assigning one-third of this group to "Negro," one-third to "Caucasian," and one-third to "Other." "Caucasian" includes Mexican-American/Spanish-American.

[e]Adjusted by rounding and adding Mexican-American/Spanish-American to "Caucasian."

[f]Adjusted by rounding; adding one-half of "Other" to "Negro" because of black response to that term; and adding American Indian to "Other."

[g]The 5 percent in the "Other" category has been added to Cross's reporting of this comparative Guidance and Placement Program data.

Table 7-7.   Enrollment of 1966-67 SCOPE College Freshmen by Race and by Degree Level of Institution

Degree Level	Caucasian	Negro	American Indian	Oriental	Mexican-American/ Spanish-American
Less than 2 Years	.02	.07	.09	.02	.09
2 Years, less than 4 Years	.33	.30	.47	.50	.70
4 Years, B.A.	.15	.31	.17	.05	.08
More than 4 Years, M.A.	.22	.15	.14	.16	.08
More than 4 Years, Ph.D.	.27	.16	.12	.27	.05
Total	1.00	1.00	1.00	1.00	1.00

Table 7-8. Educational Aspirations of 1969 SCOPE Seniors by Race

Race	STATE	High School Only	Some College	4-year Graduate	Post-graduate	Total
California						
Caucasian		.11	.29	.39	.21	1.00
Negro		.17	.28	.31	.24	1.00
American Indian		.36	.35	.17	.12	1.00
Oriental		.09	.22	.40	.29	1.00
Mexican-American/ Spanish-American		.20	.40	.28	.12	1.00
Other		.21	.39	.26	.14	1.00
Illinois						
Caucasian		.18	.24	.41	.17	1.00
Negro		.21	.34	.31	.14	1.00
American Indian		.43	.35	.17	.05	1.00
Oriental		.44	.25	.21	.10	1.00
Mexican-American/ Spanish-American		.28	.40	.17	.15	1.00
Other		.35	.33	.25	.07	1.00
Massachusetts						
Caucasian		.15	.20	.44	.21	1.00
Negro		.48	.24	.17	.11	1.00
American Indian		.35	.37	.20	.08	1.00
Oriental		.38	.31	.19	.12	1.00
Mexican-American/ Spanish-American		.32	.29	.30	.09	1.00
Other		.29	.26	.33	.12	1.00
North Carolina						
Caucasian		.16	.20	.43	.21	1.00
Negro		.48	.24	.17	.11	1.00
American Indian		.35	.37	.20	.08	1.00
Oriental		.39	.30	.19	.12	1.00
Mexican-American/ Spanish-American		.32	.29	.29	.10	1.00
Other		.29	.26	.33	.12	1.00

figure remains the same for Massachusetts and drops significantly in North Carolina [U.S. Department of Commerce and U.S. Department of Labor [1971].[2]

RACIAL DIFFERENCES IN EDUCATIONAL ASPIRATION

The racial upheaval of the 1960s was more of a revolution of rising expectations than a revolution of actual change. No doubt as expectations rise, tolerance for

2. The drop from 23 percent black enrollment (1967 SCOPE) to 15 percent (1970 HEW) is large enough to suggest that HEW figures did not include the two-year industrial institutes.

continued oppression drops and, violently or nonviolently, actual change is effected. By this reasoning, the educational aspirations of racial minorities should far outstrip their actual enrollments—and they do.

The percentage enrollments for varying degree levels have been given by racial distribution for the 1966–67 SCOPE college freshmen. A switch is now made to the 1969 SCOPE seniors to assess the educational aspirations which were not available by race in the sample of 1966 SCOPE seniors. This will be done by state since the racial composition of the four sample states is quite different.

The differences by state in Table 7-8 are as notable as the differences by race. California, with its 92–plus public community colleges, has markedly lower percentages of seniors who do not anticipate going to college. California, with its 19 large state colleges and its 9 university campuses, has the highest percentages (except for Mexican-Americans) of students planning on post-graduate degrees. In general, it appears that the level of educational aspiration in a state corresponds to the level of collegiate opportunity in that state.

As to racial differences, the following generalizations appear to be justified by the figures: the black students in California have ambitions that at least equal those of the white students (this is not true in North Carolina and Massachusetts but is closer to being true in Illinois); the American Indians are more likely to be content with junior college or no college; the Mexican-American students in California and Illinois are less aspiring than the black students although the rising militancy of the Mexican-American is likely to change this picture rapidly; the Oriental students in California have an even higher expectancy than the white students. This last generalization is not true in any other state which may find its explanation in the long tradition of free, or at least low-cost, public higher education in California. Orientals, as an ethnic group, highly value education, and when it is available they take advantage of it.

So, in summary, it appears that postsecondary education in these sample states both reflect the American dilemma and offer a glimmer of hope that the barrier of racial discrimination in education is beginning to be breached. Of course, tests of aptitudes and records of achievement have historically been barriers to advancement through higher education. They have also been used to shunt people into various educational tracks. The relationship of aptitude test scores and past academic achievement will be the next subject explored.

Chapter Eight

Academic Ability

Academic ability tests were devised as a means to predict "success" at some higher level of schooling. Success is defined in terms of grades; hence, for high school seniors academic ability scores are supposed to be predictive of grades that will be received in college. For a long time it has been known that for many individuals such ability tests are poor predictors of either achievement or persistence in college. Ability test scores, on the average, correlate with college achievement at about .50. Even combining ability test scores and high school grades only improves the correlation of either single measure with first semester college grades by the magnitude of .05 to .10 [Spindt 1959]. Because a correlation of .50 improves the betting odds over pure chance by 25 percent or less, some writers have suggested that such predictors should be put on the shelf along with the crystal ball and the Ouija board [Carlborg 1968]. Not so: these predictions continue to be used because they are quite successful in channeling groups in ways that many colleges highly approve of, and they continue to influence students' self-estimates which, of course, contributes toward fulfilling the prediction which they purport to make.

Whereas the quality of tests and the understanding of their proper use have steadily increased, modest predictability continues to result, in part, from the narrowness of criteria of success in college and the generally low reliability of those used—namely, grades and persistence data. Although attitudes and practices in the use of tests for guidance and selection are changing, Wesman's [1953] comment is still appropriate:

> For the counselor, they offer increased ability to estimate his client's general chances of success in an educational or vocational pursuit. For the admission officer in a college, better forecasts of dropout rate, as well as more informed selection, are possible. [P.10]

FIRST OBSERVATIONS ON ACADEMIC ABILITY

The Academic Ability Test was administered to 33,344 of the 1966 SCOPE seniors. This instrument, developed by Educational Testing Service, gives both a measure of verbal and of mathematical ability [Educational Testing Service 1964]. The combined scores are reported as they fell along a normative continuum marked off in eight equal parts (octiles). So, in the tables that follow, column one represents those students who had scores within the top 12.5 percent, whereas column eight represents those students who had scores within the bottom 12.5 percent.

Academic ability test scores may be too one-dimensional to work well in assessing an individual, but they do work in separating groups of young people from one another. The scores of youngsters in one state are higher (lower) than the scores of youngsters in another state. More young men than young women achieve high scores. The scores of those who go to college are markedly higher than the scores of those who do not. The universities, particularly the independent ones, get most of the high scorers, while the junior institutions, particularly the public ones, get more of the low scorers.

Among various colleges and universities, the range of mean scores on measures of academic ability is truly remarkable. Such diversity of ability in

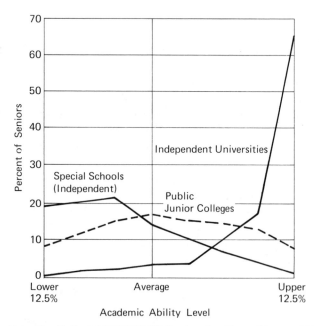

Figure 8-1. Selective Pull of 1966 SCOPE Seniors by Three Types of Postsecondary Institutions from High School Pool of Academic Ability (Four States)

student bodies was earlier demonstrated by Darley's important study of ability and achievement in higher education. By using American Council on Education (ACE) scores or their equivalents, he found that "the lowest school in [his] sample had an average rank of one; the highest school's average was equivalent to a percentile rank of 92" [Darley 1962, pp. 25-26].

A confirmation of Darley's findings is indicated by the comparative distribution of academic ability scores for students from the two most different institutional types in the SCOPE Project, namely, the private Ph.D.-granting universities and the less-than-two-year special schools. The "normative shadow" in Figure 8-1 shows the distribution for junior college students in this study.

GROUP DIFFERENCES IN ACADEMIC ABILITY

Predicting from academic ability how an individual will fare in college is un-reliable, to say the least, but what happens to different ability groups is just about what one might guess. For example, among students with academic ability scores in the highest quartile, only 15 percent opted not to enroll in college, whereas 77 percent of students with academic ability scores in the lowest quartile did not enter any form of postsecondary education. Another example using the composite four-state sample: only 5.5 percent of SCOPE seniors who did not plan to go and, indeed, did not go to college had academic ability scores in the top quartile, while 59 percent of those who enrolled in four-year colleges or universities had ability scores falling within the top quartile.

Table 8-1 gives the distribution of academic ability for each post-secondary outcome by state. It is instructive to look first at the bottom row where the composite distribution is recorded. Since there are eight subdivisions, the statistical expectancy would be 12.5 percent in each octile. California comes very close to this expectancy. Illinois and Massachusetts are low on the low end and high on the high end. North Carolina shows quite a different distribution: very high on the low side (over 50 percent in the bottom three octiles) and very low on the high side (only 26 percent in the top three octiles).

Table 8-1 shows several other notable group differences. The academic ability distribution of the "no plan/no go" subgroup is almost the reverse of the ability distribution of the senior colleges group. The distribution of those going to junior colleges is most like a cross-cut of the general population. Among the group who did not go to college, the "planned to go" subgroup is distinguishable from the "no plan/no go" subgroup. There is, of course, a piling up of high-ability scores among the senior college group in all states, and only North Carolina has as high as 15 percent of the senior college population falling below average in academic ability.

There is no such piling up of high-ability scores among the junior college group. In California and North Carolina, over 50 percent of the SCOPE seniors who enrolled in community colleges were below average in academic

Table 8-1. Distribution of Academic Ability of SCOPE Seniors (N = 33,281) With Different Postsecondary Outcomes (by State)

Postsecondary Outcomes	Academic Ability																	
	California									Illinois								
	1[a]	2	3	4	5	6	7	8[b]	Total	1	2	3	4	5	6	7	8	Total
No College — No Plan To Go	.02	.04	.08	.09	.14	.19	.22	.22	1.00	.02	.04	.08	.11	.16	.23	.20	.16	1.00
College Planned To Go	.06	.08	.10	.12	.12	.17	.18	.17	1.00	.07	.09	.12	.13	.16	.19	.14	.10	1.00
Special Schools	.02	.01	.06	.14	.09	.22	.24	.22	1.00	.03	.06	.12	.12	.15	.28	.15	.09	1.00
Junior Colleges[c]	.08	.11	.15	.15	.15	.15	.15	.06	1.00	.11	.17	.15	.16	.16	.12	.08	.05	1.00
Senior Colleges	.40	.21	.16	.09	.07	.05	.01	.01	1.00	.36	.22	.16	.12	.07	.05	.02	.00	1.00
All Students	.14	.12	.12	.11	.13	.13	.14	.11	1.00	.16	.13	.13	.13	.13	.15	.10	.07	1.00

	Massachusetts									*North Carolina*								
No College No Plan To Go	.02	.05	.09	.11	.16	.22	.22	.13	1.00	.01	.02	.05	.07	.11	.20	.23	.31	1.00
College Planned To Go	.07	.11	.13	.14	.14	.19	.13	.09	1.00	.02	.05	.06	.08	.11	.17	.19	.32	1.00
Special Schools	.03	.14	.14	.11	.15	.19	.14	.10	1.00	.02	.03	.05	.10	.15	.21	.21	.23	1.00
Junior Colleges[c]	.06	.14	.19	.19	.17	.15	.07	.03	1.00	.03	.08	.13	.17	.17	.20	.13	.09	1.00
Senior Colleges	.46	.25	.15	.07	.04	.02	.01	.00	1.00	.26	.22	.16	.12	.10	.06	.05	.03	1.00
All Students	.20	.16	.14	.11	.11	.12	.10	.06	1.00	.08	.09	.09	.10	.12	.16	.16	.20	1.00

[a]Highest octile or top 12.5 percent.
[b]Lowest octile or bottom 12.5 percent.
[c]Defined as two years, less than four years.

Table 8-2. Distribution of Academic Ability of SCOPE Seniors (N = 33,281) with Different Postsecondary Outcomes (by State and by Sex)

Postsecondary Outcomes		Academic Ability																	
		California									Illinois								
		1[a]	2	3	4	5	6	7	8[b]	Total	1	2	3	4	5	6	7	8	Total
No College — No Plan To Go	M	.04	.05	.10	.09	.12	.21	.19	.20	1.00	.03	.06	.08	.10	.15	.22	.20	.16	1.00
	F	.00	.02	.06	.10	.15	.18	.26	.23	1.00	.02	.03	.08	.12	.16	.24	.21	.14	1.00
No College — Planned To Go	M	.09	.09	.13	.11	.13	.15	.15	.15	1.00	.08	.11	.13	.15	.14	.19	.11	.09	1.00
	F	.04	.07	.08	.12	.12	.20	.19	.18	1.00	.04	.08	.12	.12	.18	.19	.15	.12	1.00
Special Schools	M	.00	.25	.25	.00	.00	.00	.00	.50	1.00	.04	.10	.24	.10	.19	.04	.19	.10	1.00
	F	.00	.00	.06	.14	.09	.23	.25	.23	1.00	.01	.06	.09	.12	.15	.33	.15	.09	1.00
Junior Colleges[c]	M	.11	.13	.14	.14	.14	.13	.16	.05	1.00	.14	.18	.15	.16	.15	.12	.06	.04	1.00
	F	.04	.10	.14	.13	.17	.20	.14	.08	1.00	.08	.15	.15	.17	.17	.13	.10	.05	1.00
Senior Colleges	M	.52	.21	.11	.06	.04	.04	.01	.01	1.00	.42	.22	.15	.10	.05	.04	.01	.01	1.00
	F	.29	.23	.19	.11	.10	.05	.02	.01	1.00	.30	.21	.18	.14	.09	.06	.02	.00	1.00
All Students	M	.18	.13	.13	.11	.12	.13	.11	.09	1.00	.20	.15	.13	.12	.11	.13	.09	.07	1.00
	F	.09	.11	.12	.12	.14	.16	.15	.12	1.00	.12	.12	.13	.13	.14	.16	.12	.08	1.00

			Massachusetts									North Carolina								
No College	No Plan To Go	M	.03	.07	.12	.12	.15	.21	.20	.10	1.00	.02	.03	.05	.06	.12	.19	.22	.31	1.00
		F	.02	.04	.06	.10	.16	.23	.24	.15	1.00	.01	.02	.04	.08	.11	.19	.24	.31	1.00
	Planned To Go	M	.08	.14	.16	.16	.13	.17	.09	.07	1.00	.03	.06	.07	.09	.11	.18	.19	.27	1.00
		F	.05	.09	.10	.12	.15	.21	.16	.12	1.00	.01	.04	.06	.07	.11	.17	.20	.34	1.00
Special Schools		M	.07	.07	.14	.10	.17	.17	.21	.07	1.00	.00	.02	.06	.15	.15	.26	.26	.10	1.00
		F	.02	.16	.14	.11	.15	.19	.13	.10	1.00	.02	.04	.04	.09	.16	.19	.20	.26	1.00
Junior Colleges[c]		M	.07	.17	.19	.17	.18	.12	.06	.04	1.00	.03	.09	.14	.17	.18	.19	.12	.08	1.00
		F	.05	.11	.18	.21	.15	.18	.09	.03	1.00	.02	.06	.13	.18	.15	.22	.14	.10	1.00
Senior Colleges		M	.50	.26	.13	.05	.03	.01	.01	.01	1.00	.33	.24	.16	.10	.08	.04	.03	.02	1.00
		F	.42	.24	.17	.09	.05	.02	.01	.00	1.00	.19	.20	.18	.13	.11	.08	.06	.05	1.00
All Students		M	.25	.18	.14	.11	.10	.10	.08	.04	1.00	.11	.10	.10	.10	.12	.15	.15	.18	1.00
		F	.16	.13	.13	.12	.12	.15	.12	.07	1.00	.05	.07	.09	.10	.14	.16	.17	.22	1.00

[a] Highest octile or top 12.5 percent.
[b] Lowest octile or bottom 12.5 percent.
[c] Defined as two years, less than four years.

Table 8-3. Postsecondary Outcomes Compared with Levels of Academic Ability of SCOPE Seniors (N = 33,281) (by State)

	Postsecondary Outcomes											
	California						Illinois					
	No College						No College					
Academic Ability	No Plan To Go	Did Plan To Go	Spec Schls	Jr Coll[a]	Sr Coll	Total	No Plan To Go	Did Plan To Go	Spec Schls	Jr Coll[a]	Sr Coll	Total
1[b]	.03	.10	.00	.26	.62	1.00	.04	.07	.00	.12	.77	1.00
2	.08	.13	.00	.37	.42	1.00	.09	.13	.01	.21	.56	1.00
3	.13	.15	.01	.43	.28	1.00	.19	.18	.01	.19	.43	1.00
4	.17	.19	.02	.45	.17	1.00	.25	.20	.01	.21	.33	1.00
5	.23	.18	.01	.46	.12	1.00	.36	.23	.02	.20	.19	1.00
6	.28	.22	.03	.40	.07	1.00	.48	.25	.02	.13	.12	1.00
7	.32	.23	.03	.40	.02	1.00	.56	.25	.02	.11	.06	1.00
8[c]	.43	.30	.04	.22	.01	1.00	.62	.26	.02	.08	.02	1.00
All Students	.21	.19	.02	.36	.22	1.00	.30	.19	.01	.16	.34	1.00

	Massachusetts						North Carolina					
1[b]	.03	.04	.00	.06	.87	1.00	.04	.06	.02	.04	.84	1.00
2	.09	.12	.02	.15	.62	1.00	.09	.12	.01	.13	.65	1.00
3	.19	.14	.03	.23	.41	1.00	.16	.15	.01	.21	.47	1.00
4	.27	.19	.02	.28	.24	1.00	.23	.19	.02	.25	.31	1.00
5	.38	.19	.04	.25	.14	1.00	.33	.22	.03	.20	.22	1.00
6	.48	.23	.04	.20	.05	1.00	.42	.26	.03	.18	.11	1.00
7	.61	.20	.04	.12	.03	1.00	.48	.29	.03	.12	.08	1.00
8[c]	.59	.24	.04	.10	.03	1.00	.51	.36	.03	.06	.04	1.00
All Students	.27	.14	.03	.17	.38	1.00	.33	.15	.02	.24	.26	1.00

[a] Defined as two years, less than four years.
[b] Highest octile or top 12.5 percent.
[c] Lowest octile or bottom 12.5 percent.

ability. Over 40 percent of the junior college students in Illinois and Massachusetts fell below average. If the "new students" will be flooding into community colleges, as several researchers predict, then these colleges are going to face an even larger problem of designing innovative and worthwhile programs for the students of modest academic ability [Cross 1971; Medsker and Tillery 1971].

When the distribution of academic ability shown in Table 8-1 is subdivided by sex, some additional group differences appear. The entire male distribution is skewed to the high side and the female distribution is skewed to the low side. This appears to be true irrespective of postsecondary outcome and is most marked at the very top and very bottom of the academic ability scale. In Table 8-2 note the bottom row in which all males are compared with all females. At the top octile of the ability scale the sex ratios by state are as follows:

California	Illinois	Massachusetts	North Carolina
$\dfrac{M}{F}$ .18 .09	$\dfrac{M}{F}$ .20 .12	$\dfrac{M}{F}$ .25 .16	$\dfrac{M}{F}$ .11 .06

In fact, the men in all states have higher percentages in the top three octiles and lower percentages in the bottom three octiles.

Among those going to senior colleges, this sex difference in measured ability is most apparent at the top octile:

California	Illinois	Massachusetts	North Carolina
$\dfrac{M}{F}$ .52 .29	$\dfrac{M}{F}$ .42 .30	$\dfrac{M}{F}$ .50 .43	$\dfrac{M}{F}$ .33 .19

Among those going to junior colleges, the sex differences are not as marked, although there is a higher proportion of men of high-measured ability and fewer of low ability when compared with women. Among those not going to college, there is only a trace of this same pattern of more men than women on the high end of the ability scale and more women than men on the low end of the scale.

Some of the group differences can be shown more dramatically when the research question is reversed to ask, "What were the postsecondary outcomes for each of the eight levels of academic ability?" The answer to this question is given in Table 8-3.

The state differences, particularly the ways in which California differs from the other three states, are eyecatching. Compare this extract of the percentage of students at the first, second, and third octile who enrolled in senior colleges in the four states:

	California	Illinois	Massachusetts	North Carolina
1st	.62	.77	.87	.84

| 2nd | .42 | .56 | .62 | .65 |
| 3rd | .28 | .43 | .41 | .47 |

And compare this extract of the percentage of students at the sixth, seventh, and eighth octile who neither planned to go nor went to any form of postsecondary institution:

	California	*Illinois*	*Massachusetts*	*North Carolina*
6th	.28	.48	.48	.42
7th	.32	.56	.61	.48
8th	.43	.62	.59	.51

It is also interesting to note that every level of academic ability is well represented in the junior colleges in California where the college door is most open. In the other three states, the students in the top octiles are more likely to enroll in the senior colleges and the students in the bottom octiles are more likely not to go to college at all. As was noted with other variables, it again appears that the group of students who planned to go to college but did not go are quite distinguishable from the "no plan/no go" subgroup. In all states, these students are well represented at every ability level except the top octile.

SELF-ESTIMATE OF PAST ACHIEVEMENT

In establishing the channels of flow from school to college, the potency of academic ability scores and high school grades goes beyond the measuring sticks of admissions officers. While in high school, students learn to judge themselves by these same measures and, when they do not measure up, they either abandon certain educational and career goals or try circuitous routes to achieve them. In recent years, such measures have even been used to legislate who goes where within state systems of colleges and universities.

One measure of academic achievement is that of students' self-reports of overall grade point average in high school. The resulting distribution of self-ratings cannot be considered the exact equivalent of actual grade point averages, although studies have shown that such distributions are highly correlated. Such self-estimates of grade point averages were used in the SCOPE Project, with results that were quite consistent with all other relevant findings:

> ITEM: Almost 80 percent of students who rated themselves as having excellent grades in high school enrolled in some postsecondary institution. Most (68 percent) of these students matriculated to four-year colleges or universities.

> ITEM: Among students who rated themselves as having poor or

Table 8-4. Self-Reported High School Grades of SCOPE Seniors (N = 16,936) Who Enrolled in Three Levels of Postsecondary Education (by State and by Sex)

Postsecondary Institutions		High School Grades									
		California					Illinois				
		Excellent[a]	Good[b]	Aver[c]	Poor– No Pass[d]	Total	Excellent[a]	Good[b]	Aver[c]	Poor– No Pass[d]	Total
Special Schools	M	.00	.50	.50	.00	1.00	.00	.29	.52	.19	1.00
	F	.00	.39	.55	.06	1.00	.02	.37	.60	.01	1.00
Junior Colleges[e]	M	.04	.38	.50	.08	1.00	.04	.33	.52	.11	1.00
	F	.05	.45	.46	.04	1.00	.05	.46	.47	.02	1.00
Senior Colleges	M	.22	.66	.11	.01	1.00	.15	.51	.31	.03	1.00
	F	.22	.64	.13	.01	1.00	.20	.59	.20	.01	1.00
All Students	M	.10	.47	.37	.06	1.00	.11	.45	.38	.06	1.00
	F	.11	.53	.33	.03	1.00	.15	.54	.30	.01	1.00

		Massachusetts					North Carolina				
Special Schools	M	.06	.16	.68	.10	1.00	.00	.16	.81	.03	1.00
	F	.01	.40	.54	.05	1.00	.05	.33	.59	.03	1.00
Junior Colleges[e]	M	.02	.29	.60	.09	1.00	.02	.22	.61	.15	1.00
	F	.03	.38	.57	.02	1.00	.04	.42	.50	.04	1.00
Senior Colleges	M	.11	.54	.32	.03	1.00	.13	.54	.31	.02	1.00
	F	.17	.60	.22	.01	1.00	.19	.60	.20	.01	1.00
All Students	M	.09	.46	.40	.05	1.00	.09	.42	.43	.06	1.00
	F	.12	.51	.35	.02	1.00	.13	.52	.33	.02	1.00

[a] Mostly A's.
[b] Mostly B's.
[c] Mostly C's.
[d] Mostly D's and F's.
[e] Defined as two years, less than four years.

not-passing grades, 77 percent did not continue beyond high school.

ITEM: Over 20 percent of this group who considered themselves as poor or not-passing did choose to go to college. Somehow, 5 percent of this low-achieving group managed to enroll in four-year colleges or universities. About 16 percent of them entered junior colleges and constituted some 7 percent of the junior college student population.

ITEM: Although 45 percent of the SCOPE seniors considered themselves to be average students, 60 percent of them did not go to college.

The above items are based on the total SCOPE sample and give no breakdown by state or by sex. Such differences are presented in Table 8–4 on those SCOPE seniors who did enroll in some form of postsecondary institution. The seniors in the Project sample who did not go beyond high school graduation were omitted from this more detailed treatment of the data.

The distribution of student-reported high school grades was remarkably consistent from state to state. The percentage of girls who reported "mostly A's" was slightly but consistently higher than that reported by boys. The percentage of girls reporting "mostly B's" was much higher than the percentage reported by boys. Since the overall distribution of grades roughly described a normal curve, it follows that more boys than girls reported "mostly C's" and also "mostly D's and F's." The superiority of girls over boys on self-reported high school grades is inconsistent with the ascendancy of boys over girls in tested academic ability and in self-estimated ability to do college-level work. To be sure, these slight differences in the academic area may actually reflect sex differences in personality traits such as those of conformity (high school grades) and cautiousness (self-estimate of ability).

Predictably, the students entering senior colleges reported the highest percentage of "excellent" grades. The surprising factor is how low, not how high, this percentage is. Even in California, where the state university system restricts admission to students in the top 12.5 percent of their senior class, only 22 percent of men and women entering senior colleges reported high school grades as "mostly A's." The other three states had lower percentages in this regard. Of course, all states had high percentages of "good" grades within these senior college groups. In Illinois, Massachusetts, and North Carolina, among the students entering senior colleges, the percentages of "average" grades were greater than the percentages of "excellent" grades.

The junior colleges in all four states enrolled more SCOPE seniors who had "poor/no pass" grades than students with "excellent" grades. Even so, from 80 to 90 percent of those entering junior college reported high school grades in the "average" (Mostly C's) or "good" (mostly B's) categories. While

Table 8–5. Comparison of Percentages of SCOPE Seniors Falling in Each Quartile of Tested Ability and Self-Estimated Ability (by State)

State		High	Above Average	Below Average	Low	Don't Know	Total
California	Tested	.26	.23	.26	.25	––	1.00
	Self-Estimated	.31	.48	.05	.01	.15	1.00
Illinois	Tested	.29	.26	.28	.17	––	1.00
	Self-Estimated	.32	.45	.07	.03	.13	1.00
Massachusetts	Tested	.37	.24	.23	.16	––	1.00
	Self-Estimated	.36	.42	.06	.03	.13	1.00
North Carolina	Tested	.17	.19	.28	.36	––	1.00
	Self-Estimated	.28	.44	.08	.02	.18	1.00

this last fact is quite consistent with the self-estimate of ability made by junior college students, it reflects higher achievement than the test scores of academic ability would predict.

SELF-ESTIMATE OF COLLEGE ABILITY

Realistic planning for any future enterprise requires a rather accurate self-estimate of one's ability to handle that enterprise. Realistic career decisions or educational planning presupposes realistic self-assessment of ability. When asked to rate themselves on ability to do college work, many SCOPE seniors demonstrated a remarkable uncertainty about their mental potential. About 15 percent of the 1966 SCOPE seniors simply responded that they didn't know whether they had or did not have the ability to do college work. This was over and beyond the rather large number who made no response to the item.

If the Academic Ability Test can be used as a validity criterion, many SCOPE seniors also demonstrated that they were as inaccurate in judging their aptitude as they were uncertain about it. In every state, 75 percent or more of the students said they "probably have" or "definitely have" the ability to do college work. This uncertainty and this inaccuracy of self-estimates of ability is underscored in Table 8–5 by comparing tested ability with self-estimate of ability.

Table 8-6. Self-Estimate of Academic Ability of SCOPE Seniors (N = 32,824) with Different Postsecondary Outcomes (by State)

Self-Estimate of College Ability

Postsecondary Outcomes		Definitely Have	Probably Have	Probably Don't Have	Definitely Don't Have	Total[a]
		California				
No College	No Plan To Go	.15	.44	.13	.04	.76
	Planned To Go	.28	.51	.05	.01	.85
Special Schools		.12	.49	.13	.02	.76
Junior Colleges[b]		.30	.54	.03	.00	.87
Senior Colleges		.55	.39	.01	.00	.95
All Students		.31	.48	.05	.01	.85
		Illinois				
No College	No Plan To Go	.10	.41	.16	.07	.74
	Planned To Go	.25	.50	.09	.02	.86
Special Schools		.11	.51	.10	.03	.75
Junior Colleges[b]		.30	.54	.03	.01	.88
Senior Colleges		.53	.40	.00	.00	.93
All Students		.32	.45	.07	.03	.87
		Massachusetts				
No College	No Plan To Go	.13	.41	.14	.07	.75
	Planned To Go	.25	.49	.09	.03	.86
Special Schools		.24	.50	.10	.03	.87
Junior Colleges[b]		.30	.54	.03	.01	.88
Senior Colleges		.60	.35	.01	.00	.96
All Students		.36	.42	.06	.03	.87
		North Carolina				
No College	No Plan To Go	.11	.40	.14	.05	.70
	Planned To Go	.24	.48	.07	.02	.81
Special Schools		.12	.50	.10	.03	.75
Junior Colleges[b]		.25	.54	.05	.01	.85
Senior Colleges		.55	.39	.00	.00	.94
All Students		.28	.44	.08	.02	.82

[a]Does not include "don't know" responses.
[b]Defined as two years, less than four years.

In the top quartile, the percentage who estimates that they belong there is quite close to the percentage who test out at that level. At the second quartile, the percentage of estimated ability is about twice as high as the percentage of tested ability. In the bottom two quartiles, the comparisons become absurd. Not many SCOPE seniors were willing to say that they "probably do not have" or "definitely do not have" the ability to do college-level work. And, no doubt, they are right. There are hundreds of thousands of students who test below average in academic ability yet perform quite well in the academic arena. Perhaps this generation of students has a more discriminating perception of college in that they are aware of different types of colleges and different programs within colleges to match the different types of students [Collins 1969].

Certainly most SCOPE seniors who enrolled in senior colleges registered confidence in their academic ability. As can be seen in Table 8-6, from 93 to 96 percent of these students estimated that they "probably have" or "definitely have" the required academic ability. Note that few, if any, were willing to say that they "probably don't have" or "definitely don't have" college-level ability. They were much more prone to give a "don't know" answer.

Table 8-6 demonstrates the truth of this last point not only for those in senior colleges but for all postsecondary outcomes. Even the "no plan/no go" group had a very small percentage who were willing to say that they "definitely don't have" the ability to handle college work.

Very few state differences are reflected in Table 8-6. Even though there are some differences in tested academic ability among states, the students' self-estimates of ability deviate very little by state. This is true whether the comparisons are among the composite of all students or by postsecondary outcomes. The only state difference worth noting is that the percentage of North Carolina junior college students who state that they "definitely have" college ability is lower than in the other three states.

The differences in the self-estimates between the two subgroups of SCOPE seniors who did not enroll in college is notable. About 25 percent of the "no plan/no go" subgroup responded with "don't know" answers, and another 17 to 23 percent of this subgroup admitted to deep doubts about their academic ability. The other subgroup, "planned to go but did not go," has a distribution pattern that is much more like the group who enrolled in junior colleges. For this subgroup, the "don't know" responses are closer to 15 percent, the self-doubting answers range from 6 to 12 percent, and the optimistic self-estimates are above 70 percent in all four states. Again, it appears that those who planned to go to college but did not go make up the most promising recruitment pool for junior colleges. One other point: those enrolling in special schools are very close in self-estimate of ability to those who neither planned to go nor went to college.

Sex differences in self-estimate of academic ability parallel the sex differences in tested ability. This can be seen by comparing Table 8-7 with

Table 8-7. Self-Estimate of Academic Ability of SCOPE Seniors (N = 32,824) with Different Postsecondary Outcomes (by State and by Sex)

Postsecondary Outcomes		Self-Estimate of College Ability									
		California					Illinois				
		Definitely Have	Probably Have	Probably Don't Have	Definitely Don't Have	Total[a]	Definitely Have	Probably Have	Probably Don't Have	Definitely Don't Have	Total[a]
No College — No Plan To Go	M	.17	.42	.12	.04	.75	.13	.39	.16	.06	.72
	F	.12	.46	.14	.05	.77	.10	.42	.16	.07	.75
No College — Planned To Go	M	.30	.47	.04	.01	.82	.30	.48	.08	.03	.89
	F	.25	.55	.06	.01	.87	.21	.52	.10	.02	.85
Special Schools	M	.25	.50	.00	.25	1.00	.10	.57	.10	.00	.87
	F	.11	.49	.14	.01	.75	.11	.56	.10	.03	.90
Junior Colleges[b]	M	.34	.51	.04	.00	.89	.36	.52	.03	.01	.92
	F	.26	.59	.03	.00	.88	.32	.57	.03	.01	.93
Senior Colleges	M	.61	.34	.01	.00	.96	.57	.37	.01	.00	.95
	F	.50	.44	.01	.00	1.00	.50	.44	.00	.00	.99
All Students	M	.35	.45	.05	.01	.86	.37	.42	.06	.00	.87
	F	.28	.52	.06	.01	.87	.28	.47	.08	.02	.86

		Massachusetts					*North Carolina*				
No College											
No Plan To Go	M	.17	.40	.14	.05	.76	.14	.39	.13	.05	.68
	F	.10	.43	.15	.09	.77	.09	.41	.15	.06	.71
Planned To Go	M	.29	.46	.07	.03	.85	.28	.43	.08	.02	.81
	F	.21	.51	.10	.04	.86	.21	.51	.07	.02	.81
Special Schools	M	.14	.45	.14	.00	.73	.07	.61	.07	.00	.75
	F	.26	.52	.09	.03	.90	.14	.54	.10	.03	.81
Junior Colleges[b]	M	.34	.50	.02	.01	.87	.27	.50	.05	.01	.83
	F	.26	.59	.03	.01	.89	.23	.57	.05	.00	.85
Senior Colleges	M	.63	.32	.00	.00	.95	.60	.34	.00	.00	.94
	F	.56	.39	.01	.00	.96	.50	.44	.00	.00	.99
All Students	M	.41	.39	.05	.02	.87	.32	.40	.07	.02	.81
	F	.30	.46	.07	.04	.87	.24	.47	.08	.02	.81

[a] Does not include "don't know" responses.
[b] Defined as two years, less than four years.

Table 8–8.   Postsecondary Outcomes Compared with the Self-Estimates of Academic Ability of SCOPE Seniors (by State)

Postsecondary Outcomes

Self-Estimate of College Ability	California						Illinois					
	No College		Spec Schls	Jr Coll[a]	Sr Coll	Total	No College		Spec Schls	Jr Coll[a]	Sr Coll	Total
	No Plan To Go	Did Plan To Go					No Plan To Go	Did Plan To Go				
Definitely Have	.10	.17	.01	.34	.38	1.00	.11	.15	.00	.17	.57	1.00
Probably Have	.19	.21	.02	.41	.18	1.00	.27	.21	.01	.19	.31	1.00
Probably Don't Have	.52	.18	.04	.21	.04	1.00	.67	.23	.02	.07	.02	1.00
Definitely Don't Have	.70	.14	.02	.11	.03	1.00	.78	.16	.01	.04	.01	1.00
All Students	.21	.19	.02	.36	.22	1.00	.30	.·		.16	.34	1.00

	Massachusetts						*North Carolina*					
Definitely Have	.10	.11	.02	.14	.63	1.00	.14	.21	.01	.13	.52	1.00
Probably Have	.27	.17	.03	.21	.31	1.00	.31	.26	.03	.32	.23	1.00
Probably Don't Have	.64	.21	.04	.07	.04	1.00	.63	.23	.03	.09	.02	1.00
Definitely Don't Have	.74	.18	.02	.05	.00	1.00	.76	.17	.02	.03	.02	1.00
All Students	.28	.15	.03	.17	.38	1.00	.34	.24	.02	.14	.26	1.00

[a]Defined as two years, less than four years.

Table 8-2. The men are more inclined to state boldly that they "definitely have" the ability. At every level of postsecondary outcome except special schools, a higher percentage of men than women said they "definitely have" college-level aptitude. The women seem more prone to cautious optimism; they say they "probably have" the ability. The women are not more disposed than men to estimate their ability below that required by college, nor are they more inclined to duck the question by answering "don't know."

Table 8-8 is a vivid illustration of the potency of self-concept. If young people think that they do not have the ability to succeed in college, then they do not go to college. Among the SCOPE seniors who estimated that they "probably don't have" college-level ability, from 70 percent (California) to 90 percent (Illinois) did not enroll in any postsecondary institution. Among those who estimated that they "definitely don't have" the ability to do college work, from 84 percent (California) to 94 percent (Illinois) did not enroll in college. Take away the junior colleges and these self-estimates become from 92 percent to 98 percent self-fulfilling prophecies. Particularly in the open-door community colleges of California, those with low self-esteem in academic pursuits were still tempted to enroll and make an effort.

These same California junior colleges attracted much higher percentages of SCOPE seniors who estimated that they "probably have" and "definitely have" the ability required by college than did the other three states. In all states, however, the effect of the junior college is to increase the number and percentage of students going to college. More often than not, this increase comes from the groups who are quite confident of their ability but, varying according to how welcome they are, those with low self-estimate of ability also swell the enrollments of the junior college.

Table 8-8 also shows that many students who are apparently confident of their academic ability do not go on to college. Between 21 percent (Massachusetts) and 35 percent (North Carolina) of the SCOPE seniors did not enroll in college even though they had the self-estimate that they "definitely have" the ability to handle college work. Among those who estimated that they "probably have" college-level ability, from 40 percent (California) to 57 percent (North Carolina) did not enter any postsecondary institution.

Perhaps financial constraints, more than lack of ability or lack of confidence in ability, keep young people out of college. Other SCOPE data shows that those with only marginal ability are the same ones who are obliged to work to support themselves. It could be that even in the late twentieth century it is social class more than ability that determines who shall and who shall not go to college. These are crucial issues, and attention will now be turned to them.

Chapter Nine

Financing a College Education: Expectation and Reality

The opportunity for higher education is not nearly as egalitarian and as merito-
cratic as the American myth would have people believe. Even when tuition is as
low as $200, only 25 percent of American families can afford it, and only 4
percent can meet the entire cost of sending their children to colleges with
tuition in the $3,000 range [Collins 1970]. It is ironic but true that at every
level of higher education, including the low-cost community college, those who
are poorer subsidize the children of those who are richer. For example, University
of California students (U.C.) during the mid-1960s averaged $5,000 in public
subsidy (actual operational cost per student minus tuition paid by the student),
state college students (S.C.) averaged $3,800 in public subsidy, junior college
students (J.C.) averaged $1,000 in public subsidy, and the 40 percent of
California youth who did not go to any college got $0 in public subsidy. The
average incomes of the parents of each student group were $12,000+ (U.C.),
$10,000 (S.C.), and $8,500 (J.C.) [Hansen and Weisbrod 1969]. "Thus, the
average subsidy received at U.C. is 30 percent greater than that received by S.C.
students and 400 percent greater than the J.C. subsidy—in spite of the fact that
'need,' as reflected by family income, runs in the opposite direction" ["The
Equality Fiction." *New Republic,* 1969, Vol. 161, pp. 23-24]. [New Republic,
September 6, 1969, p. 23].

  For a student, financing his education is a crucial issue in deciding
whether to enroll and continue in college. SCOPE data shows that while many
plus factors may dispose a high school senior to attend college, an unfavorable
financial expectation certainly is one of the major deterrents. The SCOPE data
relates in detail the college choice, student expectations for financial support,
and the students' actual financial support to these two variables: family income
level and academic ability. Expectations were ascertained from the SCOPE
seniors in 1966. Data on actual financial support was secured in 1967 from those
SCOPE students who did enroll in some postsecondary institution.

Table 9-1.   Family Income of SCOPE Seniors (N = 33,965)
Compared to AAT Quartiles

Family Income	Ability Level				
	Bottom Quartile	Third Quartile	Second Quartile	Top Quartile	Total
Much Higher	.12	.21	.24	.43	1.00
Higher	.14	.23	.27	.36	1.00
Average	.26	.30	.23	.21	1.00
Lower	.34	.29	.20	.17	1.00
Much Lower	.42	.25	.17	.16	1.00

FAMILY INCOME AND ACADEMIC ABILITY

Table 9-1 documents the general relationship between family income and scholastic ability as measured by the Academic Ability Test. The single largest group of SCOPE seniors in the top ability quartile of their graduating class came from families in the highest category of reported income. Conversely, an equally large proportion of SCOPE seniors in the lowest ability quartile came from families in the lowest category of reported income.

Further, it is apparent that while nearly two out of three students from higher-than-average-income families attend college, that ratio is reversed for students from lower income families.

INFLUENCE OF COST AND FINANCIAL AID ON COLLEGE DECISION

The 1966 SCOPE seniors were asked to rate the influence that the cost of college and the availability of financial aid had on their decisions concerning

Table 9-2.   Comparison of College-Goers and Non-College-Goers
Among SCOPE Students (N = 33,965) by Family Income

Education	Family Income		
	Lower	Average	Higher
College	.39	.47	.66
Noncollege	.61	.53	.34
Total	1.00	1.00	1.00

college. The students were simply asked to rate whether the factor had a major influence, a minor influence, or no influence on their decisions.

Table 9-3 shows how students with different postsecondary outcomes rated low cost as an influence in their decision regarding college. The percentages are given for each of the four states and are computed by sex. Actually, there do not appear to be many differences among states, and the differences by sex do not fall into any discernible pattern. At the very most, only a quarter of the students were willing to dismiss cost as having no influence. Those most inclined to say that cost was a minor rather than a major influence were the students who enrolled in senior colleges. Even in Massachusetts, where college costs are rather steep, only 33 percent of the men and 37 percent of the women rated cost as a major influence.

Table 9-4 records by postsecondary outcome the percentage of SCOPE seniors who rated the availability of financial aid as having a major, minor, or no influence on their decision regarding college. The Californians were least concerned about financial aid, and the North Carolinians were most concerned. Again, those going to senior colleges appeared to be the most affluent and least concerned about securing financial aid. The sex differences were not notable, and the only state difference worth mention is the more cavalier attitude registered by the California junior and senior college students. Although the influence of both cost and availability of financial support was rated higher by students who did not go to college, the difference in the pattern of response between college-goers and noncollege-goers was not as great as expected.

PARENTAL SUPPORT

SCOPE data reveals a marked contrast between student expectations of parental support and the actual support received. Table 9-5 documents the expectation of SCOPE seniors regarding financial support. More than one-third of students from the highest income group expected their families to pay for the total cost of their college education. Conversely, among students from the lowest income families, 43 percent expected their parents to contribute nothing at all toward their college expenses. These 1966 expectations of SCOPE seniors were generally borne out in the 1967 actuality of SCOPE college freshmen. This can be seen by comparing Table 9-5 with Table 9-6. Note, for example, that among students from families with a much-higher-than-average income, 34 percent expected and 37 percent received more than $1,800 per year. By way of contrast, among students in the lower-than-average income groups, 88 percent of the families contributed either less than $600 or nothing at all. Students from families falling in the two lower income brackets tended to expect more than they got at the high end and got more than they expected at the low end. Thus, it appears that the higher the parental income, the more likely the children will go to college,

Table 9-3. Influence of Cost as a Factor in College Choice by Different Postsecondary Outcomes (N = 29,303) (by State and by Sex)

Postsecondary Outcomes		Low Cost: Influence on College Choice							
		California				Illinois			
		Major	Minor	None	Total	Major	Minor	None	Total
No College — No Plan To Go	M	.44	.39	.17	1.00	.48	.33	.19	1.00
	F	.47	.36	.17	1.00	.49	.38	.13	1.00
No College — Planned To Go	M	.49	.39	.12	1.00	.46	.42	.12	1.00
	F	.43	.41	.16	1.00	.44	.42	.14	1.00
Special Schools	M	.75	.00	.25	1.00	.39	.50	.11	1.00
	F	.33	.41	.26	1.00	.41	.47	.12	1.00
Junior Colleges[a]	M	.49	.40	.11	1.00	.49	.39	.12	1.00
	F	.49	.37	.14	1.00	.40	.46	.14	1.00
Senior Colleges	M	.33	.43	.24	1.00	.32	.45	.23	1.00
	F	.30	.46	.24	1.00	.34	.44	.22	1.00
All Students	M	.45	.40	.15	1.00	.41	.41	.18	1.00
	F	.42	.40	.18	1.00	.41	.42	.17	1.00

		Massachusetts				North Carolina			
No College									
No Plan To Go	M	.42	.37	.21	1.00	.47	.38	.15	1.00
	F	.43	.41	.16	1.00	.50	.38	.12	1.00
Planned To Go	M	.41	.41	.18	1.00	.51	.37	.12	1.00
	F	.40	.42	.18	1.00	.43	.42	.15	1.00
Special Schools	M	.41	.38	.21	1.00	.47	.38	.15	1.00
	F	.29	.50	.21	1.00	.34	.52	.14	1.00
Junior Colleges[a]	M	.42	.44	.14	1.00	.47	.42	.11	1.00
	F	.36	.44	.20	1.00	.43	.41	.16	1.00
Senior Colleges	M	.33	.41	.26	1.00	.37	.45	.18	1.00
	F	.37	.38	.25	1.00	.42	.44	.14	1.00
All Students	M	.38	.41	.21	1.00	.44	.41	.15	1.00
	F	.38	.41	.21	1.00	.44	.42	.14	1.00

[a]Defined as two years, less than four years.

Table 9-4. Influence of Financial Aid as a Factor in College Choice by Postsecondary Outcomes (N = 29,260) (by State and by Sex)

Postsecondary Outcomes		Financial Aid: Influence on College Choice							
		California				Illinois			
		Major	Minor	None	Total	Major	Minor	None	Total
No College	No Plan To Go								
	M	.33	.35	.32	1.00	.38	.36	.26	1.00
	F	.32	.31	.37	1.00	.42	.37	.21	1.00
	Planned To Go								
	M	.28	.33	.39	1.00	.31	.32	.37	1.00
	F	.25	.37	.38	1.00	.34	.33	.33	1.00
Special Schools	M	.25	.25	.50	1.00	.28	.22	.50	1.00
	F	.34	.27	.39	1.00	.29	.38	.33	1.00
Junior Colleges[a]	M	.25	.34	.41	1.00	.32	.29	.39	1.00
	F	.22	.31	.47	1.00	.29	.30	.41	1.00
Senior Colleges	M	.24	.27	.49	1.00	.29	.27	.44	1.00
	F	.21	.26	.53	1.00	.28	.28	.44	1.00
All Students	M	.26	.33	.41	1.00	.32	.30	.38	1.00
	F	.25	.30	.45	1.00	.33	.32	.35	1.00

		Massachusetts				North Carolina			
No College / No Plan To Go	M	.42	.32	.26	1.00	.44	.35	.21	1.00
	F	.49	.34	.17	1.00	.46	.34	.20	1.00
No College / Planned To Go	M	.37	.30	.33	1.00	.41	.31	.28	1.00
	F	.39	.30	.31	1.00	.40	.33	.27	1.00
Special Schools	M	.31	.31	.38	1.00	.37	.32	.31	1.00
	F	.35	.37	.28	1.00	.26	.33	.41	1.00
Junior Colleges[a]	M	.30	.34	.36	1.00	.30	.33	.37	1.00
	F	.27	.35	.38	1.00	.29	.34	.37	1.00
Senior Colleges	M	.32	.27	.41	1.00	.36	.27	.37	1.00
	F	.32	.30	.38	1.00	.34	.32	.34	1.00
All Students	M	.34	.30	.36	1.00	.38	.31	.31	1.00
	F	.36	.32	.32	1.00	.38	.33	.29	1.00

[a]Defined as two years, less than four years.

Table 9-5. Expectations of 1966 SCOPE Seniors (N = 33,965) of Parental Support for College Costs by Family Income

Family Income	Expected Parental Contribution					
	None of Cost	1/4 of Cost	1/2 of Cost	3/4 of Cost	All of Cost	Total
Much Higher	.12	.11	.16	.27	.34	1.00
Higher	.16	.18	.22	.23	.21	1.00
Average	.24	.23	.21	.17	.15	1.00
Lower	.34	.25	.18	.12	.11	1.00
Much Lower	.43	.27	.15	.08	.07	1.00

the more likely the parents will foot the students' out-of-pocket costs, and the more likely society will subsidize the remaining costs.

Many studies, prior to and in addition to the SCOPE Project, have demonstrated the relationship between high family income and high performance on academic achievement tests. At this point, consideration will be turned to the financial expectation of students grouped by ability level as well as contrasted by high and low family income. Half of the students in the top ability group from low-income families expect to receive no support at all from their families; a total of 80 percent of students from low-income families expect to receive no more than one-fourth of their expenses or nothing at all. In contrast, among high-ability students in the highest-income families, 66 percent expect either three-fourths support or total support. Table 9-8 shows that these 1966 expectations are essentially correct although there is a tendency to underestimate parental help at both the very high and the very low end.

Table 9-6. Parental Support to 1967 SCOPE College Students (N = 10,590) by Family Income

Family Income	Amount of Financial Support from Parents					
	$0	$600 or less	$601–1,200	$1,201–1,800	More than $1,800	Total
Much Higher	.08	.25	.15	.15	.37	1.00
Higher	.12	.40	.18	.13	.17	1.00
Average	.16	.51	.18	.09	.06	1.00
Lower	.23	.56	.13	.04	.04	1.00
Much Lower	.30	.58	.07	.03	.02	1.00

Table 9–7. Expectations of 1966 SCOPE Seniors (N = 33,965) of Parental Support for College Costs (by High and Low Family Incomes Within Each AAT Quartile[a])

Ability Level	Income Bracket	Expected Parental Contribution					
		None of Cost	*1/4 of Cost*	*1/2 of Cost*	*3/4 of Cost*	*All of Cost*	*Total*
Top Quartile	Low	.52	.28	.09	.07	.04	1.00
	High	.07	.10	.17	.33	.33	1.00
Second Quartile	Low	.44	.33	.13	.07	.03	1.00
	High	.11	.10	.16	.27	.36	1.00
Third Quartile	Low	.45	.29	.11	.09	.06	1.00
	High	.17	.10	.15	.21	.37	1.00
Bottom Quartile	Low	.35	.22	.23	.09	.11	1.00
	High	.26	.17	.14	.15	.28	1.00

[a]Income classifications were based on student reporting during the senior year of high school of family income level in relation to a national average of $6,200. Of the five possible classifications (N = 33,965), this table deals only with subjects who reported "Much higher" (N = 3,613) or "Much lower" (N = 1,321) family incomes than average.

Table 9-8. Parental Support to 1967 SCOPE College Students (N = 10,590) (by High and Low Family Incomes Within Each AAT Quartile[a])

Ability Level	Income Bracket	Amount of Financial Support from Parents					
		$0	$600 or less	$601– 1,200	$1,201– 1,800	More than $1,800	Total
Top Quartile	Low	.39	.51	.06	.02	.02	1.00
	High	.06	.18	.16	.16	.44	1.00
Second Quartile	Low	.30	.56	.08	.04	.02	1.00
	High	.11	.35	.12	.14	.28	1.00
Third Quartile	Low	.23	.67	.06	.03	.01	1.00
	High	.09	.40	.17	.13	.21	1.00
Bottom Quartile	Low	.20	.68	.07	.05	.00	1.00
	High	.22	.41	.12	.10	.15	1.00

[a]Income classifications were based on student reporting during the senior year of high school of family income level in relation to a national average of $6,200. Of the five possible classifications (N = 10,590), this table deals only with subjects who reported "Much higher" (N = 1,669) or "Much lower" (N = 335) family incomes than average.

Table 9-9. Expectations of 1966 SCOPE Seniors (N = 33,965) of Financial Support Through Paid Work (by Family Income)

Family Income	*Portion of Cost to be Defrayed by Paid Work*					
	None of Cost	*1/4 of Cost*	*1/2 of Cost*	*3/4 of Cost*	*All of Cost*	*Total*
Much Higher	.51	.34	.08	.03	.04	1.00
Higher	.39	.40	.11	.05	.05	1.00
Average	.35	.38	.14	.06	.07	1.00
Lower	.33	.39	.13	.06	.09	1.00
Much Lower	.30	.41	.13	.07	.09	1.00

FINANCIAL SUPPORT FROM PAID WORK

SCOPE seniors, regardless of socioeconomic background, seemed to make a realistic estimate of the proportion of college costs that could be met through part-time work. Very few, even in the lowest-income family groups, expected to earn total support for themselves by working. As is shown in Table 9-9, most of the seniors, even those from low-income families, expected that working while in college would provide one-fourth or less of the cost.

The seniors' 1966 expectations were borne out in 1967 actuality. Note in Table 9-10 how very few students in any family income category actually reported earnings of more than $600 during the freshman year. More students with lower family incomes are obliged to work and earn are than

Table 9-10. Financial Support to 1967 SCOPE College Students (N = 10,590) Earned Through Paid Work (by Family Income)

Family Income	*Amount of Earned Financial Support*					
	$0	*$600 or less*	*$601– 1,200*	*$1,201– 1,800*	*More than 1,800*	*Total*
Much Higher	.70	.27	.01	.01	.01	1.00
Higher	.62	.34	.02	.01	.01	1.00
Average	.57	.38	.03	.01	.01	1.00
Lower	.53	.42	.03	.01	.01	1.00
Much Lower	.51	.45	.03	.01	.00	1.00

Table 9-11. Expectations of 1966 SCOPE Seniors (N = 33,965) of Financial Support Through Paid Work (by High and Low Family Incomes Within Each AAT Quartile[a])

Ability Level	Income Bracket	Portion of Cost To Be Defrayed by Paid Work					
		None of Cost	1/4 of Cost	1/2 of Cost	3/4 of Cost	All of Cost	Total
Top Quartile	Low	.23	.51	.13	.07	.06	1.00
	High	.50	.40	.05	.02	.03	1.00
Second Quartile	Low	.33	.42	.12	.06	.07	1.00
	High	.52	.33	.08	.03	.04	1.00
Third Quartile	Low	.32	.40	.12	.06	.10	1.00
	High	.53	.27	.09	.05	.06	1.00
Bottom Quartile	Low	.32	.36	.13	.08	.11	1.00
	High	.44	.20	.18	.08	.10	1.00

[a]Income classifications were based on student reporting during the senior year of high school of family income level in relation to a national average of $6,200. Of the five possible classifications (N = 33,965), this table deals only with subjects who reported "Much higher" (N = 3,604) or "Much lower" (N = 1,309) family incomes than average.

Table 9-12. Financial Support to 1967 SCOPE College Students (N = 10,590) Earned Through Paid Work (by High and Low Family Incomes Within Each AAT Quartile[a])

Ability Level	Income Bracket	Amount of Earned Financial Support					
		$0	*$600 or less*	*$601–1,200*	*$1,201–1,800*	*More than $1,800*	*Total*
Top Quartile	Low	.48	.48	.03	.01	.00	1.00
	High	.73	.26	.01	.00	.00	1.00
Second Quartile	Low	.48	.50	.02	.00	.00	1.00
	High	.67	.30	.02	.00	.01	1.00
Third Quartile	Low	.46	.47	.07	.00	.00	1.00
	High	.68	.28	.03	.01	.00	1.00
Bottom Quartile	Low	.73	.15	.02	.00	.00	1.00
	High	.71	.29	.00	.00	.00	1.00

[a]Income classifications were based on student reporting during the senior year of high school of family income level in relation to a national average of $6,200. Of the five possible classifications (N = 10,590), this table deals only with subjects who reported "Much higher" (N = 1,665) or "Much lower" (N = 333) family incomes than average.

**Table 9-13.   Expectations of 1966 SCOPE Seniors (N = 33,965)
of Financial Support Through Savings (by Family Income)**

	Portion of Cost To Be Covered Through Savings					
Family Income	None of Cost	1/4 of Cost	1/2 of Cost	3/4 of Cost	All of Cost	Total
Much Higher	.49	.33	.09	.04	.05	1.00
Higher	.39	.38	.12	.06	.05	1.00
Average	.32	.37	.16	.07	.08	1.00
Lower	.33	.35	.15	.08	.09	1.00
Much Lower	.32	.37	.14	.08	.09	1.00

students with higher family incomes but, as Table 9-10 reveals, earning one's
way through college is more myth than reality.

The difficulty, as was suggested in Table 9-1, is that high family
income and high ability tend to go together so that students who are obliged to
work are often those least able to carry this additional burden. Table 9-11 makes
this point. Half of the high-ability students from the lowest-income group
expect to earn up to 25 percent of the cost of their college education. On the
other hand, half of the high-ability students from the highest-income group do
not expect to work at all. In actuality, SCOPE data indicates that of the 1967
college students who did work part-time, the ratio of low-income families to
high-income families was about five to three. The notable exception was in
the low-ability group. Perhaps these students learned the hard way that they
could not work and at the same time survive in college.

**Table 9-14.   Financial Support to 1967 SCOPE College Students
(N = 10,590) From Savings (by Family Income)**

	Financial Support Available from Savings					
Family Income	$0	$600 or less	$601– 1,200	$1,201– 1,800	More than $1,800	Total
Much Higher	.39	.49	.11	.01	.00	1.00
Higher	.31	.55	.11	.02	.01	1.00
Average	.31	.58	.09	.02	.00	1.00
Lower	.29	.62	.08	.01	.00	1.00
Much Lower	.26	.65	.08	.01	.00	1.00

Table 9-15. Expectations of 1966 SCOPE Seniors (N = 33,965) of Financial Support Through Loans (by Family Income)

Family Income	Expectation Regarding Loans		
	Will Probably Apply for Loan	Will Not Apply for Loan	Total
Much Higher	.22	.78	1.00
Higher	.34	.66	1.00
Average	.40	.60	1.00
Lower	.46	.54	1.00
Much Lower	.52	.48	1.00

The conclusions to be drawn about working while in college are the following: First, students do not expect to "work their way through college"; they expect to earn about one-fourth of their expenses. Second, actuality confirms the students' expectations. Third, the ratio of low-income to high-income students who do work while in college is about five to three.

Table 9-16. Expectations of 1966 SCOPE Seniors (N = 33,965) of Financial Support Through Loans (by High and Low Family Incomes Within Each AAT Quartile[a])

Ability Level	Income Bracket	Expectation Regarding Loans		
		Will Probably Apply for Loan	Will Not Apply for Loan	Total
Top Quartile	Low	.57	.43	1.00
	High	.23	.77	1.00
Second Quartile	Low	.56	.34	1.00
	High	.21	.79	1.00
Third Quartile	Low	.50	.50	1.00
	High	.20	.80	1.00
Bottom Quartile	Low	.51	.49	1.00
	High	.29	.71	1.00

[a]Income classifications were based on student reporting during the senior year of high school of family income level in relation to a national average of $6,200. Of the five possible classifications (N = 33,965), this table deals only with subjects who reported "Much higher" (N = 3,625) or "Much lower" (N = 1,440) family incomes than average.

Table 9-17. Proximity of College to Home as an Influence on Decision-Making of SCOPE Seniors (N = 29,279) with Different Postsecondary Outcomes (by State and by Sex)

Postsecondary Outcomes		Proximity to Home: Influence on College Choice							
		California				Illinois			
		Major	Minor	None	Total	Major	Minor	None	Total
No College — No Plan To Go	M	.35	.37	.28	1.00	.30	.38	.32	1.00
	F	.38	.33	.29	1.00	.29	.45	.26	1.00
No College — Planned To Go	M	.38	.43	.19	1.00	.34	.42	.24	1.00
	F	.38	.35	.27	1.00	.35	.38	.27	1.00
Special Schools	M	.50	.00	.50	1.00	.24	.41	.35	1.00
	F	.36	.42	.22	1.00	.29	.42	.29	1.00
Junior Colleges[a]	M	.46	.37	.17	1.00	.34	.39	.27	1.00
	F	.48	.34	.18	1.00	.35	.42	.23	1.00
Senior Colleges	M	.31	.36	.33	1.00	.22	.41	.37	1.00
	F	.27	.35	.38	1.00	.27	.40	.33	1.00
All Students	M	.39	.38	.23	1.00	.28	.40	.32	1.00
	F	.38	.35	.27	1.00	.31	.41	.28	1.00

		Massachusetts				North Carolina			
No College	No Plan To Go	M	.28	.38	.34	1.00	.33	.44	.23	1.00
		F	.31	.34	.35	1.00	.37	.39	.24	1.00
	Planned To Go	M	.30	.39	.31	1.00	.37	.39	.24	1.00
		F	.32	.40	.28	1.00	.33	.43	.24	1.00
Special Schools		M	.34	.38	.28	1.00	.29	.38	.33	1.00
		F	.22	.45	.33	1.00	.33	.35	.32	1.00
Junior Colleges[a]		M	.36	.40	.24	1.00	.38	.41	.21	1.00
		F	.32	.39	.29	1.00	.31	.43	.26	1.00
Senior Colleges		M	.26	.39	.35	1.00	.22	.42	.36	1.00
		F	.26	.40	.34	1.00	.23	.44	.33	1.00
All Students		M	.29	.39	.32	1.00	.31	.42	.27	1.00
		F	.29	.40	.31	1.00	.31	.42	.27	1.00

[a]Defined as two years, less than four years.

FINANCIAL SUPPORT THROUGH SAVINGS
AND LOANS

The conclusions on support through savings are similar to the conclusions about working through college. Regardless of the income group, students do not expect to finance more than a fraction of their education by savings from summer work. Seniors from lower-income groups tend to believe that a larger fraction of their expenses can be met through savings than do students from high-income groups. Again, the 1966 expectations of SCOPE seniors (Table 9-13) are consistent with the reality reported by 1967 SCOPE freshmen (Table 9-14).

If students cannot look to family, to paid work, or to savings for financial support, then the remaining alternative is to get a loan. As might be expected, there is a clear relationship between family income and a student's intention to apply for a college loan: the higher the family income, the less likely a student is to apply for such a loan, and vice versa. The intention to apply for a loan does not appear related to ability level as reflected by AAT quartiles. Students of low ability are as willing to take the risk of a loan as are students of high ability. The significant fact, shown in both Tables 9-15 and 9-16, is that the odds are better than two to one that a student who applies for a loan is from a low-income family.

PROXIMITY TO HOME AS A FINANCIAL FACTOR

To go away to college costs money, or put the other way, for many students, proximity of college to home should serve as a hidden but fortuitous subsidy. The SCOPE seniors were asked if closeness to home were a major influence, a minor influence, or an influence of no importance on their choice of a college. The results of this inquiry are shown in Table 9-17. California had the highest percentage of students rating proximity of college to home as a major influence and the lowest percentage saying it was of no importance. The reason, apparently, is the highly developed community college system in California. Close to 50 percent of the SCOPE seniors enrolled in California junior colleges had marked proximity of college to home as a major influence, and less than 20 percent said it was of no importance.

About 30 percent of all students reported that closeness of college and home was of no importance. Those who enrolled in senior colleges had a higher percentage who responded "of no importance," yet this percentage difference from the composite (norm) was not very large. Logic would suggest that the "no plan/no go" group would say that proximity was of no importance since they had no plans to go to college anyway. The facts do not bear out this logic. This group responded in much the same fashion as when all student responses are lumped together in composite form.

Again, expectancy might tempt prediction that proximity of college to home would loom larger from the feminine than from the masculine perspective. This does not appear to be the case: not for students taken as a whole, not for students who enrolled in senior colleges, not for junior college students, and not even for students who planned to go to college but did not carry through on these plans.

Considering all the data on how SCOPE seniors expect to finance college expenses, a rather gloomy picture emerges. Not many parents can afford the full costs of higher education for their children. Relatively few students seem to expect that work, or savings, or loans will provide them sufficient money to finance their college education. Proximity of college to home is a positive factor, particularly in states with highly accessible junior colleges. High-ability students from the lowest-income group—the type of student now wanted in many institutions of higher education—are, on the whole, the most pessimistic with regard to their ability to finance their college education.

Perhaps if students were to make early plans for college-going, they would have time to work out the real and fancied obstacles that they see in their path. Perhaps last-minute decisions mean that one takes what one can get; thus, early decisions greatly increase the possibilities of being selective. Both the timing of decision-making and the selectivity of college choice are factors that should be considered. These somewhat related, somewhat disparate determinants will be the next subject of inquiry and will then lead to the final determinant under consideration—guidance in the high schools.

Chapter Ten

Timing and Selectivity of Decision

One of the more promising aspects of SCOPE research concerns the timing of educational and career decisions. This timing relates to commitment as a determinant of behavior. Does early commitment to a course of action put a person on a track, so to speak, that leads to his behavioral goal? The earlier evidence presented on student fulfillment of parental aspirations and of their own aspirations suggests that, though derailment is possible, the person is likely to go down the track of expectancy. The data now to be presented gives strong corroboration to this common-sense observation. It does appear that youngsters who make early decisions to go to college do, in fact, go. Of course, this is not to argue that they go simply because they make early decisions. However, it does suggest that decision in itself may be a determinant; hence, counselors should encourage students to give early and deep exploration to educational and career decisions.

TIMING OF POSTSECONDARY DECISIONS

Table 10-1 records, for each postsecondary outcome, the percentage of students in each state who remembered late, intermediate, or early decisions on what they wanted to do after high school. Of course, some students did not know, so that is also shown as a category of response.

The early deciders are not very many—roughly 20 percent. However, they constitute considerably more than 20 percent of the SCOPE seniors who entered Ph.D.-granting institutions. Actually, about 70 percent of those entering the universities claimed either early or intermediate decisions about college. By contrast, only 10 to 16 percent of those students who enrolled in junior colleges were early deciders, and 40 percent or more of them were classified as late deciders. Surprisingly, a low percentage of those entering special schools responded, "I don't know," and a relatively high percentage of students who

Table 10-1. Timing of Decision Regarding College by SCOPE Seniors (N = 16,920) with Different Postsecondary Outcomes (by State)

Timing of Postsecondary Decisions

Postsecondary Institutions	California					Illinois				
	Late[a]	*Inter-med.*[b]	*Early*[c]	*Didn't Know*	*Total*	*Late*[a]	*Inter-med.*[b]	*Early*[c]	*Didn't Know*	*Total*
Special Schools	.39	.41	.18	.02	1.00	.46	.36	.15	.03	1.00
Junior Colleges[d]	.46	.35	.11	.08	1.00	.40	.37	.16	.07	1.00
Four Years B.A.	.24	.39	.25	.12	1.00	.26	.41	.23	.10	1.00
More Than Four Years M.A.	.27	.37	.29	.07	1.00	.28	.43	.21	.08	1.00
More Than Four Years Ph.D.	.19	.33	.37	.11	1.00	.21	.40	.29	.10	1.00
All Students	.37	.36	.19	.08	1.00	.30	.40	.21	.09	1.00

	Massachusetts					North Carolina			
Special Schools	.42	.36	.15	.07	1.00	.45	.45	.07	.03	1.00
Junior Colleges[d]	.39	.43	.13	.05	1.00	.46	.38	.10	.06	1.00
Four Years B.A.	.20	.46	.26	.08	1.00	.26	.43	.22	.09	1.00
More Than Four Years M.A.	.19	.43	.30	.08	1.00	.24	.44	.23	.09	1.00
More Than Four Years Ph.D.	.20	.41	.30	.09	1.00	.20	.39	.29	.12	1.00
All Students	.26	.42	.24	.08	1.00	.32	.41	.19	.08	1.00

[a]Twelfth grade or "haven't decided yet."
[b]Eleventh, Tenth, or Ninth grade.
[c]Eighth grade or before.
[d]Defined as two years, less than four years.

Table 10-2. Timing of Decision Regarding College by SCOPE Seniors with Different Postsecondary Outcomes (by State and by Sex)

Postsecondary Institutions		California					Illinois				
		Late[a]	Inter-med.[b]	Early[c]	Didn't Know	Total	Late[a]	Inter-med.[b]	Early[c]	Didn't Know	Total
Special Schools	M	.00	.50	.50	.00	1.00	.43	.38	.14	.05	1.00
	F	.40	.41	.17	.02	1.00	.48	.36	.15	.01	1.00
Junior Colleges[d]	M	.47	.36	.10	.08	1.00	.44	.35	.13	.08	1.00
	F	.46	.34	.13	.07	1.00	.35	.40	.19	.06	1.00
Four Years B.A.	M	.31	.35	.25	.09	1.00	.29	.42	.20	.09	1.00
	F	.18	.42	.26	.14	1.00	.22	.41	.27	.10	1.00
More Than 4 Years M.A.	M	.29	.38	.25	.08	1.00	.34	.40	.18	.08	1.00
	F	.24	.36	.32	.08	1.00	.23	.44	.24	.09	1.00
More Than 4 Years Ph.D.	M	.19	.30	.39	.12	1.00	.22	.41	.27	.10	1.00
	F	.17	.36	.37	.10	1.00	.18	.39	.33	.10	1.00
All Students	M	.39	.35	.17	.09	1.00	.32	.39	.20	.09	1.00
	F	.35	.35	.22	.08	1.00	.26	.41	.25	.08	1.00

		Massachusetts					North Carolina				
Special Schools	M	.52	.34	.07	.07	1.00	.56	.38	.06	.00	1.00
	F	.40	.37	.17	.06	1.00	.42	.48	.06	.04	1.00
Junior Colleges[d]	M	.43	.42	.09	.06	1.00	.53	.36	.06	.05	1.00
	F	.34	.44	.17	.05	1.00	.40	.41	.13	.06	1.00
Four Years B.A.	M	.26	.49	.16	.09	1.00	.31	.42	.17	.10	1.00
	F	.14	.43	.36	.07	1.00	.21	.44	.25	.10	1.00
More Than 4 Years M.A.	M	.26	.44	.22	.08	1.00	.31	.44	.17	.08	1.00
	F	.13	.42	.37	.08	1.00	.19	.43	.28	.10	1.00
More Than 4 Years Ph.D.	M	.22	.42	.27	.09	1.00	.21	.41	.27	.11	1.00
	F	.17	.39	.35	.09	1.00	.19	.37	.31	.13	1.00
All Students	M	.29	.44	.19	.08	1.00	.37	.39	.16	.08	1.00
	F	.23	.42	.28	.07	1.00	.28	.42	.21	.08	1.00

[a]Twelfth grade or "haven't decided yet."
[b]Eleventh, Tenth, or Ninth grade.
[c]Eighth grade or before.
[d]Defined as two years, less than four years.

enrolled in Ph.D.-granting universities claimed that they did not know when they had decided on their posthigh-school plans.

Table 10-2 treats the same data in the same way but subdivided by sex. Although it seems somewhat surprising, girls appear quicker to make up their minds about college than do boys. There is in each state at least a 5 percentage point differential in favor of the girls on early decisions and about the same differential for late decisions on the part of the boys. Even when the choice was for the local junior college, the girls registered a higher percentage of early decisions.

This sex difference, though inconsistent with folk myth, is consistent with traditional evidence regarding the earlier physiological and psychological development of girls when compared with boys. This data may also reflect quite different environmental pressures on the two sexes regarding life after high school. The male decision, which must accommodate educational alternatives to cultural expectations regarding economic independence and military service, is indeed complicated and influenced by future contingencies over which the student has little control. The female decision is complicated by the incongruence between early educational experiences which are generally more successful than those for boys and societal role expectations which emphasize marriage and family life.

Combined with other data in this report, these findings suggest the following normative profile of the *early deciders:*

> Although there are more girls than boys in this group, they are predominantly high ability students who have been successful in school and who share with their parents high aspirations for education beyond high school. It is not surprising, then, that they are disproportionately represented in the highly selective colleges and universities, and particularly so in the private sector of higher education.

The *late deciders,* on the other hand, generally have quite different histories and outcomes. Their normative profile might be described as follows:

> Although half of the students who went to college made late decisions about what to do after high school, boys were over-represented in this group. These students are highly diverse in reference to academic ability, educational achievement, and aspiration, but those with modest ratings on these characteristics are disproportionately represented. This fact is reflected in the high proportions of late deciders who attended the less selective institutions, particularly those which are public and of less than baccalaureate level.

Table 10–3. Percent of Early Decision-Makers Attending Different Types of Postsecondary Institutions with Ranks for Men and Women[a]

Men			*Women*	
Rank	*Percent*	*Institution by Degree Level and Control*	*Percent*	*Rank*
1	.51	Catholic Two-Year	.30	8
2	.41	Other church-related M.A.	.34	5
3	.34	Independent Ph.D.	.36	4
4	.29	Independent M.A.	.36	3
5	.28	Public Ph.D.	.33	6
6	.27	Catholic M.A.	.25	12
7	.26	Catholic Ph.D.	.31	7
8	.26	Other church-related Ph.D.	.40	1
9	.24	Independent B.A.	.38	2
10	.22	Public Two-Year	.14	16
11	.19	Other church-related B.A.	.26	11
12	.16	Public B.A.	.24	13
13	.16	Public M.A.	.28	10
14	.13	Catholic B.A.	.29	9
15	.12	Other church-related Two-Year	.20	14
16	.09	Independent less than two years	.11	17
17	.08	Independent Two-Year	.15	15
Insufficient Cases		Public less than two years	Insufficient Cases	
		Catholic less than two years		
		Other church-related less than two years		

[a]Early decision-makers were defined as students who said they made decisions about what to do after high school by grade eight or earlier.

Approximately 40 percent of the college-goers said they decided what to do after high school when they were in the ninth, tenth, or eleventh grades. These *intermediate deciders* are indeed diverse and show no consistent patterns in type of postsecondary institution chosen.

EARLY DECISION FOR WHAT?

One answer to this question is early decision for a Ph.D.-granting university. It is true that this level of postsecondary institution had a higher percentage of early deciders than any other level. Even so, every level had its early decision-makers, thereby suggesting contributing factors other than institutional level. This was confirmed when the group who claimed early decision were checked for type of collegiate institution that had attracted them. The results of this investigation are given in Table 10–3 by differentiating the types of institutions by degree level and by type of control and then reporting the percentage of early deciders who enrolled in each type. Percentages are given for men on the left side of the table and for women on the right side. The rank order by sex is also recorded.

It is apparent that the church-related colleges (Catholic and other), and the more selective public and private institutions attracted large numbers of early decision-makers. Future SCOPE publications will examine the relationship of religious orientations of students to the timing of both educational and career choice. Trent has already demonstrated the potency of religious orienta-tion to such choices [Trent with Golds 1967]. It seems likely that an equally potent influence in early choice of college is a family history of association with a specific institution. This is suggested by the high rank of independent colleges and universities which tend to have traditions of familial lineage.

THE SELECTIVE ATTRACTION OF
PRIVATE INSTITUTIONS

There are some obvious and well-documented student characteristics which are associated with success (academic achievement) in college [Sanford 1967a]. Academic aptitude, socioeconomic background, intellectual predisposition, and parental aspirations would be good examples. On nine such variables associated with success in college, the selective attraction of private institutions is apparent in the findings of the SCOPE Project.

This attraction of the "elite" is especially true of the independent colleges and universities. Compared to the public or to the denominational colleges and universities, the independents attracted a higher proportion of their students from high-income levels, from high scorers on measure of academic aptitude and intellectual predisposition, from professional and managerial families, and from students who made early decisions regarding college atten-dance. Furthermore, these students were high achievers in high school and had aspirations to attend graduate school and to enter professional and managerial careers. As might be expected, while in high school they considered themselves capable of doing college-level work in higher proportions than did any other outcome group. This pattern of selectivity holds for the independent liberal arts colleges as well as the independent university, although the percentages of elite students are generally higher at the university level.

The selective characteristics of students going to nonpublic institutions is apparent at all levels, from the less-than-two-year colleges to Ph.D.-granting universities. At each level, on most of the nine discriminating characteristics, the nonpublic students differed from their peers who selected public institutions. Not only this, but the patterns are progressive ones with higher proportions of plus items at each successive institutional level. Selectivity is, of course, most apparent at the university level. All of these generalizations are shown quantitatively in Table 10-4. Except on three items, the independent universities registered the highest proportions of favorable student characteristics of the four control types. Two of these exceptions hold special interest, however, for in both instances the Catholic institutions are the ones that score the highest percentages. On one, postgraduate aspiration, the percentage of students in independent and Catholic institutions is identical. But on high student occupational preference, there is a 3 percent margin in favor of the students in Catholic colleges, which is matched by parental aspirations for students in Catholic colleges to continue on to postgraduate education. These high aspirations may reflect aspirations of Catholic families to enter a social class status in which they have been underrepresented in the past.

Keeping in mind that universities generally attract student bodies which on the average are more academically able, have higher aspirations, have family resources for education, and are composed of students who have had wide choice of educational opportunity, it becomes quite apparent from Table 10-4 that the independent nonpublic universities are indeed skimming off the elite students from American high schools.

Certain public universities, to be sure, are unusually successful in competing for elite students although their student mix is different from the selective independent universities. Furthermore, there are state differences in this competitive game. The University of California, for example, has selective admissions policies more rigorous than most other state universities and garners a high proportion of students with these "success" characteristics.

A comparison of the percentage of elite students from each of the four project states who attended public universities is made in Table 10-5. Caution must be used, however, in interpreting apparent differences of entering students in the four state universities since both in- and out-of-state universities are reported. The data for California is least questionable because of the low out-of-state attendance by California students. Only two key variables are reported in this four-state comparison, namely, high academic aptitude and high occupational status of father.

The message is somewhat garbled, but it does appear that the University of California is the most selective of the four state university systems. A number of states, California among them, have state master plans for develop-

Table 10-4.   Selective Attraction of 'Elite' Students by Four Types of Universities (Four-State Composite)

Student Success Characteristic	Percentage of SCOPE Students Registering Success Characteristic			
	Type Institutional Control			
	Public	Catholic	Other Denominational	Independents
1. High Academic Aptitude (Upper 12%)	.48	.53	.46	.66
2. Father in Professional or Managerial Career	.50	.44	.57	.61
3. High Intellectual Predisposition (Upper 12%)	.26	.23	.26	.37
4. Definite Confidence in College Ability	.59	.70	.60	.71
5. Aspire to Postgraduate Study	.32	.45	.37	.45
6. Aspire to Professional or Managerial Career	.90	.94	.86	.91
7. Applied to 3 or More Colleges	.30	.52	.45	.68
8. Family Income Much Higher than U.S. Norm	.22	.24	.23	.28
9. Parents Want Student To Do Graduate Study	.19	.31	.23	.28

Table 10-5.   Selective Attraction of 'Elite' Students by Public Universities from Four SCOPE States

	Percentage of SCOPE Students Registering Success Characteristic			
	Public Universities			
Student Success Characteristic	*California*	*Illinois*	*Massachusetts*	*North Carolina*
1. High Academic Aptitude (Upper 12%)	.53	.44	.54	.45
2. Father in Professional or Managerial Career	.66	.50	.38	.45

ing prestigious public universities on an undergirding of only moderately selective state colleges and open-door public two-year colleges. The success of such master plans depends upon effective coordination among components of the public sector of higher education. Some competent students of higher education conclude that the central objective of such master planning, the transfer of students, is working smoothly [Willingham and Findekyan 1969]. Although the success of junior college students who transfer to the University of California is heartening [Knoell and Medsker 1964], the ratio of entering junior college students who actually transfer is surprisingly low (7 percent in 1968), and racial and ethnic groups are underrepresented among those who do transfer.

No doubt this ratio could be much improved if guidance counselors helped students and their families to understand fully how a tiered system of progressive selectivity could best be used. As a matter of fact, the proper differentiation and the equitable distribution of youth from school to college is highly dependent on the adequacy of the high school guidance program. It will be to this determinant that attention will now be turned before summing up the conclusions and implications of this aspect of the SCOPE Project.

Chapter Eleven

High School Guidance

One of the disturbing findings of the SCOPE Project was the frequent and recurring response of students that in areas of knowledge vital to decision-making, they simply did not know.

> Freedom is a function of understanding and if access to such under-standing is denied or limited, then freedom is denied or limited. . . . If a person has no knowledge, or only vague knowledge of the alternative courses of action open to him and the consequences of each alternative, then his freedom (choice to act) has been grossly abridged. [Collins 1969, p. 34]

The 1966 SCOPE seniors were asked to evaluate the helpfulness of several key areas of the high school guidance experience. From one-fifth to one-third of these seniors from the four states in the Project reported *no* counseling experiences in the eight guidance areas sampled.

STUDENT EVALUATION OF GUIDANCE

Considering the usual generosity of youth, it is not very reassuring to find that only about half of the SCOPE seniors declared that the high school guidance services were helpful. Of course, the ratings varied by counseling area. For example, only 44 percent of the students were satisfied with the counseling help they had received on study habits, whereas counseling about college aptitude tests was reported helpful by 61 percent of the seniors.

Of most concern is the evidence that a surprisingly high per-centage of the students never talked over problems in decision-making with any school person, counselor, or teacher. This is shown in Table 11-1 which displays the percentage of boys and girls who reported, on the eve of leaving high school,

Table 11-1. 'Neglected' Areas of Counseling as Reported by 1966 SCOPE Seniors (by Composite, by State, and by Sex)

Rank Order	Guidance Area	Sex	Percentage Reporting No Counseling Assistance				
			Four-State Composite	California	Illinois	Massachusetts	North Carolina
1	Applying for Jobs	M	.31	.33	.35	.37	.24
		F	.29	.36	.29	.33	.22
2	Costs of Different Schools and Colleges	M	.25	.31	.25	.26	.21
		F	.30	.36	.32	.33	.24
3	Study Habits	M	.25	.27	.27	.24	.22
		F	.31	.33	.31	.36	.26
4	College Admission, Housing, Financial Aid	M	.23	.25	.23	.22	.22
		F	.28	.29	.29	.30	.25
5	Results of Vocational Aptitude Tests	M	.23	.24	.23	.27	.18
		F	.28	.34	.29	.29	.22
6	Available Programs in Colleges and Schools	M	.18	.20	.20	.16	.16
		F	.21	.23	.24	.22	.17
7	Results of Vocational Interest Tests	M	.16	.18	.16	.20	.13
		F	.21	.27	.20	.24	.16
8	Results of College Ability Tests	M	.11	.13	.11	.11	.11
		F	.16	.19	.16	.18	.14

that they had never received counsel in the eight guidance areas shown. The areas of guidance are presented in rank order of "neglect."

To be sure, there is no basis for assuming that all students experience problems in each of these areas and therefore require counseling. For example, many college-oriented students would not be particularly interested in "Applying for Jobs" and job-oriented students would not be very interested in "College Admission, Housing, Financial Aid." Even so, it does appear that the scale of guidance functions is tipped toward the college-bound students. Note that the least neglected area of counseling was "Results of College Ability Tests." Concern with this apparent counseling emphasis would be lessened if such testing were not based upon such a narrow perception of talents beyond high school. Willingham, in his important monograph on relevance in postsecondary education, has stated the issue clearly:

> There is a great deal of evidence that traditional procedures and measures used by schools and colleges are unduly rigid in channeling talent. There is need to develop broader interpretations of talent and educational programs and to improve the connection between the two. [1969, p. 42]

Even though widespread professional counseling is a more recent development in North Carolina than in the other Project states, more students from that state reported that they had had counseling in seven of the eight guidance areas. More important, the North Carolina students reported counseling to be more helpful than their peers in the other states. The area in which there was no meaningful difference was counsel concerning the results of ability testing.

Girls reported less counseling than boys in seven of the eight guidance areas. The one guidance area with no sex difference was that of "Applying for Jobs." On the average, this difference in the reporting of no counseling experience is about 5 percentage points higher for girls. Perhaps these differences may reflect the general decline in the commitment that postadolescent girls have for education, or maybe the lesser expectations which some school people have for girls. The gathering momentum of the women's liberation movement in the last two years may have rendered both of these hypotheses irrelevant.

Note that in most of the eight guidance areas, more California and Massachusetts girls report counseling neglect than do the girls of Illinois and North Carolina. This is difficult to explain since guidance is highly professionalized in both California and Massachusetts.

GUIDANCE CONCERNING COLLEGE

High school counselors cannot take at face value students' statements that they have no plan to go to college. Some students who have no plan to go to college

Table 11-2. Evaluation of Helpfulness of High School Guidance Concerning College by SCOPE Seniors (N = 31,377) with Different Postsecondary Outcomes (by State)

Helpfulness of Guidance Concerning College

Postsecondary Outcomes	California					Illinois				
	Very Helpful	*Helpful*	*Not Helpful*	*Not Discussed*	*Total*	*Very Helpful*	*Helpful*	*Not Helpful*	*Not Discussed*	*Total*
No College No Plan To Go	.08	.26	.27	.39	1.00	.10	.25	.22	.43	1.00
No College Planned To Go	.12	.29	.25	.34	1.00	.17	.33	.23	.27	1.00
Special Schools	.16	.31	.22	.31	1.00	.08	.37	.19	.36	1.00
Junior Colleges[a]	.11	.30	.24	.35	1.00	.17	.36	.21	.26	1.00
Senior Colleges	.20	.42	.20	.18	1.00	.26	.43	.17	.14	1.00
All Students	.13	.32	.24	.31	1.00	.18	.35	.20	.27	1.00

Postsecondary Outcomes	Massachusetts					North Carolina				
	Very Helpful	*Helpful*	*Not Helpful*	*Not Discussed*	*Total*	*Very Helpful*	*Helpful*	*Not Helpful*	*Not Discussed*	*Total*
No College No Plan To Go	.09	.27	.20	.44	1.00	.16	.32	.19	.33	1.00
No College Planned To Go	.16	.35	.20	.29	1.00	.26	.35	.17	.22	1.00
Special Schools	.17	.34	.22	.27	1.00	.20	.38	.16	.26	1.00
Junior Colleges[a]	.19	.39	.18	.24	1.00	.20	.34	.19	.27	1.00
Senior Colleges	.25	.41	.18	.16	1.00	.31	.36	.16	.17	1.00
All Students	.19	.35	.19	.27	1.00	.23	.34	.18	.25	1.00

[a]Defined as two years, less than four years.

do, in fact, go. Further, the counselor has no way of knowing in advance that some students who plan to go actually do not go. The 48 percent of the SCOPE sample who did not go to college was made up of 20 percent who had no plan to go and 28 percent who planned to go, but failed to do so. Hence, all of the SCOPE seniors were asked to evaluate the helpfulness of counselors in "such things as when and how to apply for scholarships, for housing, and for admission to certain colleges." [Tillery, Donovan, Sherman pg. 14, 1966c]

The percentages of students rating this guidance area as "very helpful," "helpful," "not helpful," or "not discussed" are reported by post-secondary outcomes in Table 11-2. Naturally, those students who went to a senior college were the most generous in rating high school guidance concerning college as being helpful. Not many of the "no plan/no go" group said such guidance was "very helpful," although 25 percent or more of this group did say it was "helpful." Across the four states, the junior college group had about the same percentage ratings as the group who planned to go to college but did not go. Again, it appears that these two groups come from a common pool. Among those enrolled in senior colleges, 60 to 70 percent rated the high school guidance as "helpful" or "very helpful."

The most surprising figures in Table 11-2 are the percentages reflecting no counseling about college. More than one-third of the "no plan/ no go" group responded that factors concerning college had not been dis-cussed. From 24 to 35 percent of students enrolled in junior colleges made the same charge. Even among those in senior colleges, about 15 percent said that vital facts about college had never been discussed.

It will be recalled from Table 11-1 that the girls had a significantly higher rating of "College Admission . . . " as a neglect area of guidance. When this evaluation is parsed out by a different postsecondary outcome, it becomes clear that this sex difference is most pronounced among the girls who do not go to college (see Table 11-3). There is no appreciable sex difference in the ratings on helpfulness of counselors among students enrolled in senior colleges. The notable difference is in the "no plan/no go" group where up to 50 percent of the girls (Massachusetts) say that facts about college admissions were not discussed.

So, essentially, what was found in this inquiry on the helpfulness of guidance in regard to college admissions? The answer, collapsed into composite percentages, is shown graphically in Figure 11-1. About 40 percent of those students going to senior college rated the counseling they had received as being "helpful," and another 26 percent said it was "very helpful." The respective percentages dropped to 34 percent "helpful" and 16 percent "very helpful" for those going to junior colleges and for those who planned to go to college but did not go. For the "no plan/no go" group the percentages again dropped to 28 percent "helpful" and 12 percent "very helpful." About 20 percent of the

Table 11-3.   Evaluation of Helpfulness of High School Guidance Concerning College by SCOPE Seniors with Different Postsecondary Outcomes (by State and by Sex)

Postsecondary Outcomes		Helpfulness of Guidance Concerning College									
		California					Illinois				
		Very Help-ful	Help-ful	Not Help-ful	Not Dis-cussed	Total	Very Help-ful	Help-ful	Not Help-ful	Not Dis-cussed	Total
No College	No Plan To Go										
	M	.09	.26	.30	.35	1.00	.12	.23	.27	.38	1.00
	F	.08	.25	.23	.44	1.00	.09	.26	.19	.46	1.00
	Planned To Go										
	M	.11	.31	.27	.31	1.00	.18	.31	.26	.25	1.00
	F	.13	.27	.24	.36	1.00	.16	.35	.20	.29	1.00
Special Schools	M	.00	.75	.00	.25	1.00	.05	.35	.25	.35	1.00
	F	.17	.29	.23	.31	1.00	.10	.37	.17	.36	1.00
Junior Colleges[a]	M	.12	.30	.25	.33	1.00	.17	.36	.21	.26	1.00
	F	.10	.31	.23	.36	1.00	.18	.36	.21	.25	1.00
Senior Colleges	M	.23	.42	.18	.17	1.00	.27	.43	.16	.14	1.00
	F	.20	.41	.21	.18	1.00	.26	.43	.18	.13	1.00
All Students	M	.13	.32	.25	.30	1.00	.19	.34	.22	.25	1.00
	F	.13	.32	.22	.33	1.00	.17	.35	.19	.29	1.00

		Massachusetts					North Carolina				
No College	No Plan To Go	M	.10	.28	.26	.36	1.00	.16	.33	.21	.30	1.00
		F	.08	.25	.17	.50	1.00	.16	.31	.17	.36	1.00
	Planned To Go	M	.16	.36	.22	.26	1.00	.26	.32	.21	.21	1.00
		F	.18	.33	.17	.32	1.00	.26	.38	.14	.22	1.00
Special Schools		M	.36	.42	.18	.04	1.00	.16	.46	.15	.23	1.00
		F	.14	.32	.22	.32	1.00	.22	.35	.16	.27	1.00
Junior Colleges[a]		M	.20	.37	.19	.24	1.00	.22	.30	.22	.26	1.00
		F	.18	.41	.18	.23	1.00	.19	.37	.17	.27	1.00
Senior Colleges		M	.27	.39	.18	.16	1.00	.30	.35	.17	.18	1.00
		F	.23	.44	.18	.15	1.00	.33	.36	.15	.16	1.00
All Students		M	.20	.36	.21	.23	1.00	.23	.34	.19	.24	1.00
		F	.17	.34	.18	.31	1.00	.24	.36	.16	.24	1.00

[a]Defined as two years, less than four years.

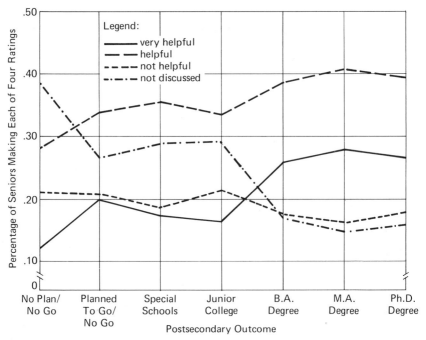

Figure 11-1. Percentage of Responses on Four Ratings of Counselor's Helpfulness with College Admissions (N = 31,377)

sample, irrespective of postsecondary outcome, rated the counseling about college admissions as being "not helpful."

The most dramatic contrast is found in comparing the "no plan/ no go" group with the senior college group on the percentage reporting "not discussed." Almost 40 percent of the seniors who neither planned to go nor went to college said that college admissions had never been discussed with them. Another 21 percent of this group reported that the discussion they had had was "not helpful." As has been shown in previous chapters of this report, this group has a concentration of the poor, the undereducated, the ethnic minorities— the losers in this society. If the high school guidance function, wittingly or unwittingly, is to divert these young people from the college channel, then current guidance practices should be applauded for successful cost-benefit analysis. If, on the other hand, guidance should provide new awareness of postsecondary opportunities for the economically and socially disadvantaged, then the innocent-looking lines in Figure 11-1 represent a serious indictment.

One other point on guidance concerning college: it is a popular notion and frequently asserted that high school students turn to their teachers, rather than to their counselors, for advice concerning college. The author, in his article

Table 11–4. Evaluation of Helpfulness of High School Guidance Concerning Applying for Work by SCOPE Seniors (N = 31,429) with Different Postsecondary Outcomes (by State)

Helpfulness of Guidance Concerning Applying for Work

Postsecondary Outcomes	California					Illinois				
	Very Helpful	Helpful	Not Helpful	Not Discussed	Total	Very Helpful	Helpful	Not Helpful	Not Discussed	Total
No College — No Plan To Go	.20	.28	.12	.29	1.00	.30	.32	.18	.20	1.00
No College — Planned To Go	.14	.25	.26	.35	1.00	.22	.31	.22	.25	1.00
Special Schools	.13	.39	.26	.22	1.00	.28	.31	.20	.21	1.00
Junior Colleges[a]	.11	.24	.26	.39	1.00	.14	.29	.22	.35	1.00
Senior Colleges	.05	.15	.24	.56	1.00	.08	.23	.22	.47	1.00
All Students	.12	.23	.25	.40	1.00	.18	.28	.21	.33	1.00

Postsecondary Outcomes	Massachusetts					North Carolina				
	Very Helpful	Helpful	Not Helpful	Not Discussed	Total	Very Helpful	Helpful	Not Helpful	Not Discussed	Total
No College — No Plan To Go	.30	.32	.17	.21	1.00	.40	.33	.11	.16	1.00
No College — Planned To Go	.21	.29	.21	.29	1.00	.41	.31	.12	.16	1.00
Special Schools	.21	.39	.18	.22	1.00	.35	.36	.11	.18	1.00
Junior Colleges[a]	.14	.27	.24	.35	1.00	.25	.31	.16	.28	1.00
Senior Colleges	.05	.19	.22	.54	1.00	.14	.26	.17	.43	1.00
All Students	.16	.26	.21	.37	1.00	.31	.31	.13	.25	1.00

[a]Defined as two years, less than four years.

Table 11-5. Evaluation of Helpfulness of High School Guidance Concerning Applying for Work by SCOPE Seniors with Different Postsecondary Outcomes (by State and by Sex)

		Helpfulness of Guidance Concerning Applying for Work									
		California					Illinois				
Postsecondary Outcomes		Very Helpful	Helpful	Not Helpful	Not Discussed	Total	Very Helpful	Helpful	Not Helpful	Not Discussed	Total
No College — No Plan To Go	M	.14	.26	.29	.31	1.00	.22	.29	.23	.26	1.00
	F	.25	.32	.17	.26	1.00	.35	.33	.15	.17	1.00
No College — Planned To Go	M	.13	.26	.29	.32	1.00	.18	.29	.26	.27	1.00
	F	.16	.24	.23	.37	1.00	.27	.33	.17	.23	1.00
Special Schools	M	.25	.50	.25	.00	1.00	.15	.10	.45	.30	1.00
	F	.13	.38	.26	.23	1.00	.31	.36	.14	.19	1.00
Junior Colleges[a]	M	.09	.23	.29	.39	1.00	.10	.28	.25	.37	1.00
	F	.13	.26	.23	.38	1.00	.20	.29	.18	.33	1.00
Senior Colleges	M	.04	.15	.28	.53	1.00	.07	.20	.25	.48	1.00
	F	.06	.15	.20	.59	1.00	.09	.26	.19	.46	1.00
All Students	M	.09	.24	.29	.39	1.00	.13	.26	.25	.37	1.00
	F	.14	.25	.21	.40	1.00	.23	.30	.17	.30	1.00

		Massachusetts					North Carolina				
No College	No Plan To Go M	.20	.30	.24	.26	1.00	.35	.34	.14	.17	1.00
	F	.37	.34	.11	.18	1.00	.45	.33	.08	.14	1.00
	Planned To Go M	.17	.29	.23	.31	1.00	.37	.31	.15	.17	1.00
	F	.26	.30	.18	.26	1.00	.44	.31	.11	.14	1.00
Special Schools	M	.28	.36	.18	.18	1.00	.31	.41	.12	.16	1.00
	F	.19	.40	.18	.23	1.00	.36	.35	.10	.19	1.00
Junior Colleges[a]	M	.15	.27	.23	.35	1.00	.25	.31	.18	.26	1.00
	F	.12	.28	.26	.34	1.00	.24	.32	.14	.30	1.00
Senior Colleges	M	.06	.19	.24	.51	1.00	.13	.25	.19	.43	1.00
	F	.05	.19	.20	.56	1.00	.16	.27	.15	.42	1.00
All Students	M	.12	.24	.23	.39	1.00	.28	.30	.16	.26	1.00
	F	.20	.27	.18	.35	1.00	.34	.31	.11	.24	1.00

[a]Defined as two years, less than four years.

"Will the Real Guidance Counselor Please Stand Up?" used 1966 SCOPE data
at every high school grade level to disprove this contention [Tillery 1969–70].
The 1966 seniors were asked whom they had consulted before choosing a
college and to name the person who had been most helpful in this decision-
making. Sixty-five percent of the SCOPE seniors said that they had not consulted with their high school teachers. Sadly, yet in sharp contrast, 43 percent
said they had not discussed this choice with their high school counselors.
Finally, when asked to name the most helpful person whom they had consulted
about the choice of college, the percentage responses were as follows:

Parents	.43
Counselors	.22
Other students	.16
Teachers	.10
College admissions officers	.09

GUIDANCE CONCERNING APPLYING FOR WORK

One of the questions posed to the SCOPE seniors was an inquiry on the helpfulness of guidance regarding "How to apply for jobs and how to act in job
interviews." Later, the responses were tabulated on the basis of postsecondary
outcome, and the results are reported by state in Table 11–4. Some 28 percent
of the 1966 SCOPE seniors neither planned to go nor went to college. The
question concerning applying for work was, of course, most relevant to this "no
plan/no go" group. Their responses differed markedly from state to state. The
"very helpful" response ranged from only 20 percent in California to 40 percent
in North Carolina. The state differences do not disappear, or even diminish, when
the responses of "very helpful" and "helpful" are collapsed into a single plus
meaning: California had 48 percent plus responses, Illinois and Massachusetts
had 62 percent favorable, and North Carolina had 73 percent on the plus
side. The same pattern of state differences applies to the group who planned to
go to college but did not carry through on their plans. In California, 35 percent
of this group said that they had never discussed applying for work with a
counselor or any other school official. In Illinois and Massachusetts, about 50
percent said that guidance on work application either had never been discussed
or, if it had, was "not helpful." In North Carolina, only 26 percent made these
negative responses.

For those going to senior colleges, it is understandable that 50
percent, on an average, would never have discussed work application. This
percentage is not so high for the junior college group (about 34 percent), but
even the lower figure is not so understandable. Many junior college students do
work while going to school, and many others drop out to work full-time shortly
after enrollment, hence they could really profit from high school guidance on

the world of work. The same criticism applies in respect to the senior college group, though to a lesser degree. Only in North Carolina did as high as 40 percent of the senior college group rate the high school guidance they received about work as being at all helpful.

Table 11–5 gives this same information but adds the further dimension of sex. Read first in composite form, Table 11–5 does show the girls reporting a much higher percentage of "very helpful" responses. This is true in every state, and the sex difference in each case is large enough to be statistically significant. The obverse of this result is also true: fewer girls than boys rated the guidance on job application as "not helpful."

The sex difference in ratings is most dramatic in the case of the

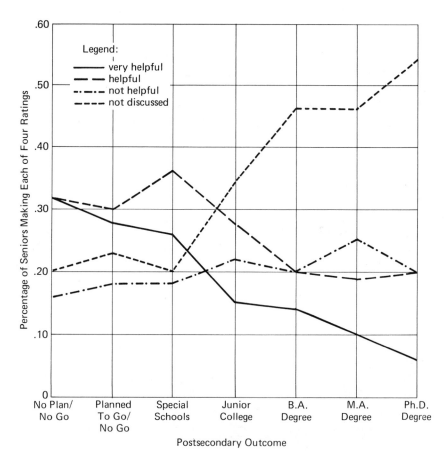

Legend:
——— very helpful
— — helpful
—·—·— not helpful
— — — not discussed

Postsecondary Outcome

Figure 11–2. Percentage of Responses on Four Ratings of Counselor's Helpfulness with Job Applications (N = 31,429)

"no plan/no go" group. Perhaps the girls were more definite that they were not going to college, and the counselors responded accordingly with advice on job application. Or perhaps the girls exhibited more initiative—or maybe more dependency—and thereby did get more help from the counselors. Whatever the reason, the sex difference also obtained for the group who planned to go to college but did not go, and in a less marked and more variable way, for all other postsecondary outcome groups except that of special schools where the number is too small to make the seeming contradiction significant.

Again, it is helpful to collapse all this data on helpfulness of guidance in regard to work application and to show the broad findings in graphical form. This is done in Figure 11-2 with rather striking results. About 80 percent of students not entering accredited colleges did discuss work application with their counselors and roughly 60 percent of this three-way grouping ("no plan/no go," "planned/but no go," and special schools) reported that the counseling was "helpful" and/or "very helpful." Nearly 35 percent of the junior college students and from 45 to 55 percent of the senior college students claimed that work application had never been discussed. Among junior college students who did discuss entry into the job market, only 15 percent found the discussion "very helpful" and 28 percent reported it "helpful." Even these low percentages drop progressively with higher and more selective levels of senior colleges.

Chapter Twelve

Educational Rites of Passage

Crises in the human life cycle—birth, puberty, marriage, death—are occasions in all societies for ritual and ceremony. Such rites of passage reduce the disrupting effects of changes in status and social relations—effects which at each crisis disturb the life of society, as well as that of the individual.

The transition of young Americans from school to college or other outcomes involves two educational rites of passage which, because of their inequities, may disturb the social order more than serve it: they are the near-universal rites of separation from high school and the more highly discriminating rites of incorporation into college life.

For over three-quarters of the young people in this country, high school graduation is a ceremony of separation from institutionalized childhood. State differences, if not regional differences, are reflected in the high school graduation rates for the SCOPE states as shown in Table 12-1. These data carry the message that even in the 1970s a shocking number of boys and girls drop out of school without ceremony, and those who do are generally the least prepared personally and educationally to face the pressures of adult life.

Even for the majority, the spring rites of separation mask the doubts and fears of the adolescent identity crisis. It is a strange festival, and behind the traditional oratory and social whirl can be observed the vastly different experiences that various groups of students are having as they make or acquiesce to decisions about the future. Whether the comparison is boys versus girls, or students with high educational aspiration versus those with low aspirations, or youngsters from poor families versus the rich, or black versus white, or even among students from states with differing educational opportunities, important differences in the decision-making process and its outcomes are to be found.

A strange loss of confidence seems to characterize young women as they approach graduation. Even though they have made much better grades in school than have boys, they are less likely to feel that they definitely have the

Table 12-1. High School Graduation Rates, 1968

Sex	State					
	California	Illinois	Massachusetts	North Carolina	Total U.S.
Male	76.2	71.8	79.0	62.7	74.2
Female	79.8	78.0	92.3	64.6	77.8
Total	78.0	74.9	85.6	66.0	76.0

Source: Adapted from the working papers of Gus. W. Haggstrom for the Carnegie Commission on Higher Education, 1970.

ability to do college work. (With the SCOPE seniors of 1966, this group comprised from 26 to 35 percent.) They report less encouragement from their parents than do boys, and when asked to identify the one most likely reason that they might not go to college, nearly half of them reported, "My parents don't think I should." Only 5 percent of the boys singled out this barrier to college attendance and, in contrast to girls, identified cost of college as the primary barrier. And, although 75 percent of both boys and girls in the SCOPE sample were located in their first-choice colleges, the two sexes chose quite differently among the types of institutions in American higher education.

Even more notable differences in the decision-making process were apparent among students from various family backgrounds. Students from homes of high-economic status make much earlier decisions about what they will do after high school than do students from working class families. They have had access to more information about educational opportunities than their less fortunate peers have had, and they have had earlier and more satisfying discussions with both counselors and teachers about education after high school.

What students do after high school is highly congruent with the expectations of their parents, and, in turn, parental expectations are clearly related to social stratification. As noted in Chapter 5, approximately half of the students from the four SCOPE states who did not plan to go to college and in fact *did not* go, said at the close of the senior year that their parents expected them only to finish high school. These students were predominantly from working class families. In contrast, over 90 percent of the students who later went to Ph.D.-granting institutions had parents who expected them at least to graduate from college. These students were primarily from professional and managerial families. About two-thirds of the 1966 SCOPE seniors who planned to go to college but did not actually reported that their parents expected them to go no further than junior college, if that. The modal family occupational status for these boys and girls was middle level.

Attitudes about self, education, and career of these students from different family backgrounds differ so markedly that they seem to represent self-fullfillment prophecies. However, two other rather contrary findings also emerge from this study: first, many young people who seem to have everything going for them drop out between school and college; and second, many others have higher educational aspirations than do their peers with similar family backgrounds. Why have students in the first group been turned off? How can this second group whose aspirations may exceed predictions best be served in school and college?

The problem of dropout between school and college of high-ability students has long concerned educators and researchers. In 1955, Flynt found that among seniors in the top ability quartile only 50 percent actually went to collage [Flynt 1955]. About a decade later, in a more select group of states, to be sure, the SCOPE follow-up revealed that approximately 15 percent of those in the upper-ability quartile did not enter postsecondary education. Since the SCOPE ratio of college to noncollege outcomes was near the national average for 1966 (slightly over 50 percent for all students), it appears that there has been a marked improvement in the continuing education of bright students. But undeveloped talent is still a national loss, particularly when it is also noted that 25 percent of the students in the upper quartile of measured intellectual predisposition did not enroll in college. In seeking to explain this underdevelopment of talent, we can turn to some evidence showing that economic barriers have been overrated. For example, some 30 percent of the students from families of high economic status did not attend college, and this is true of nearly 40 percent of those students who reported their family income to be much higher than the national average. Perhaps more central to this problem is the difficulty that many young people have in resolving the adolescent identity crisis. Erikson [1959] suggests that this crisis is resolved by achieving a sense of continuity with the past and the future. The crisis of having to choose among alternative beliefs and occupations seems a necessary state in human development. It is suggested that among those students who run counter to predictions about college-going are those who leave school in a state of identity diffusion, a state in which commitments to both the past and the future are nebulous or lacking.

Such students, whether in school or in college, need opportunities to get close to adults whose values and humanity come through. They need relationships that nurture self-understanding and identification. Some students find such relationships and models in school; other do not. Individuals who are deprived of such opportunities both at school and at home frequently have difficulty choosing among alternatives and then committing themselves to such choices. Data about this development crisis is beginning to suggest new understandings. For example, although most high school students report their teachers to be fair and their counselors helpful, they find both to be directive and conventional. Furthermore, fewer low-aspiration students than high-aspiration students turn to either teachers or counselors for help. Even when they do, they find these school people, like their parents, to be less helpful than do their peers who expect to continue their education beyond high school. More than any other groups of students, they turn more to friends of the opposite sex for help [Tillery, Donovan, and Sherman 1968]. For the poor, the black, and those with language handicaps, there is strong evidence of selective barriers to effective counseling, to access to information about opportunities beyond high school, and to maturing relationships with school personnel. The rites of separation for these young people in need are frequently painful. They have realized that their prospects may be bleak; most students leave school wanting help as they plan for the future. Over two-thirds of the 1966 SCOPE seniors said that they wanted help, and almost the same percentage of these 34,000 students called for more counseling time. It is noted sadly that some 20 percent of these students said that no one is helpful to them.

Certainly separation from high school had different meanings for that half of the highschool graduates who did not go to college than for those who did. There are convictions about education in this society that inflict damage to self-esteem when the decision is made not to enter college. For example, all but 5 percent of the 1966 California seniors reported in the spring of their senior year that they believed one needed to go to college in order to get ahead, and that their parents generally shared this conviction. They sensed, perhaps only vaguely, what Trow [1967] described in this compelling way: "One of the gains of higher education is an increased belief in one's own capacities to handle broad responsibilities, contribute to the solution of important problems, have an impact on the larger society." And again, understanding "the relation of cause and effect in social life is only one, though an important, part of (higher education's) contribution to the individual's sense of himself as the kind of person who can intervene to shape the course of events beyond the boundaries of his immediate milieu" [Ibid.] . The label of college student is so potent in certain urban youth groups that rather large numbers of students register in the local junior college without ever attending classes. They gain the status they need by the gesture of registration alone.

The *rites of transition* from school to college and from school to instant adulthood would appear to be quite different. Furthermore, the very stages of psychosocial development seem to be different for those who go to college in contrast to those who may lose their youth and enter the world of work and family life. Keniston points out that youth may be a luxury and is not available to all.

> Today, for the first time, we have a large group of people who are psychological adults and sociological adolescents. Modern society really is changing the life cycle in terms of adding new stages of development. In the Middle Ages, infancy ended at age seven. You began to work or were apprenticed out. Adolescence itself is a very recent discovery—100 years old at most. . . . The college or graduate student is very different from the early adolescent in terms of psychology and the issues with which he is concerned. It's a new stage of life and represents a further postponement of full adulthood. . . . It's a kind of apprenticeship for adulthood.[Keniston 1968, p. 23]

The boys and girls who go directly into jobs or assume family responsibilities may be so deprived. Half of the young people, then, may miss the cycle of youth during which one has the opportunities to develop a sense of power and hope and an opportunity to try to change society.

Many college-goers, on the other hand, enter a new stage of life that is a further postponement of full adulthood. Keniston sees the college student as a psychological adult and sociological adolescent. However useful this observation is, it does not seem to fit the activist students who seek to bring the world, as they see it, onto the campus and to make higher education relevant to real life.

Although it is tempting to follow Keniston's perception of the college experience as an apprenticeship for adulthood, it is also more than that. The college experience would seem to encompass a critical stage of development in its own right. Tussman, in seeing college as the setting for a crucial rite of passage, claims that "college is the most crucial of battlefields. . . . It is not simply that it is a place of confrontation—youth and age, feeling and habit, impulse and discipline, innocence and experience. It is the place where the essential vitality of the society is tested—its capacity to claim and harness the energy and commitments of its youthful self. The society brings itself, in the college, to public trial" pg. 1 [Tussman 1968]. Whereas Tussman sees college as the point at which society comes to self-consciousness, it is—perhaps for that very reason—also the focus of the identity crisis for many youth. The traditional rites of passage from school to college seem to have little relevance for the central problems of helping students find environments in which identity and commitment are enhanced.

The decision-making process about college and career has been the primary focus of the SCOPE Project. The data, when pieced together, lead to increased convictions about the centrality of student identity formation. Integral to a student's identity is his relationship with significant persons in his life and his assessment of their expectations for him. What has been learned about differences in the quality, direction, and timing of identification patterns should enhance understanding and improve prediction about the decisions that students make concerning education and career.

Marcia [1966] has suggested an interesting way of grouping young people in reference to identity status during adolescence. Some students have achieved identity by committing themselves to the choices they have made among occupational and ideational alternatives. They seem able to make it, so to speak, and have self-confidence as they face the future. No doubt many of the early decision-makers will fall into this group. These students are attracted in large numbers to competitive and elite colleges.

Other students seem to have "foreclosed" in identity development. They seem to have accepted what others expect of them (their parents primarily) and seem not to have experienced a period of choice. Their faith is literally that of their fathers, and college choice is a confirmation of childhood beliefs. Although these young people are found in all types of colleges, they tend to avoid controversial or avant garde institutions.

Two other subgroups of students have been identified by Marcia— those in a state of deferred identity and those who might be described as having identity diffusion. Students in the first group are actively examining fundamental beliefs and are almost preoccupied with making choices. They are not quite independent of plans that their parents have for them. In brief, students who are at this stage while in high school would seem to be testing their beliefs against alternative choices of colleges and careers.

Students in the final group have not made many occupational or ideational decisions and aren't much concerned. They lack commitments and are no doubt to be found among those who do not attend college but who have the means and abilities to do so.

Perhaps the convictions that young people have about their abilities to succeed in college are even more related to identity status. Here again, the differences for outcome groups are marked. This relationship between such self-confidence and outcome after high school has been demonstrated in this study.

Although Cross [1971], in her book on the new students in higher education, documents the steady increase in college attendance by children from families of low socioeconomic status, it is doubtful that any segment of education substantially serves the poor, regardless of color. Willingham observes "that inequities in opportunity are so imbedded in the American culture that substantial change will require great effort" [Willingham 1970, p. 2]. The inequities in educational opportunities from birth on, which are associated with ethnic-racial origins and economic status, can scarcely be overcome by bargain-counter education nor an academic pecking order that penalizes the many for the few.

The human potentials for learning are almost boundless; the possibilities for turning students on, almost untapped; the vital forces of self-identity motivation, too often ignored—all this in the final quarter of the twentieth century. America is on the threshold of having the resources and interlocking talents in all our schools and colleges to make education work for everyone. Perhaps what is still lacking most is that balance of heart and mind which is essential to unconditional regard for the individuality and developmental potential of the young people to be served.

References

"A Conversation with Kenneth Keniston on The Psychology of Student Activists" by Mary Harrington Hall, *Psychology Today,* November 1968, Vol. 2, No. 6, pp. 16–23.

American Council on Education. 1969. *A Fact Book on Higher Education.* Washington, D.C.: ACE.

American Council on Education. 1967. *A Fact on Higher Education.* Washington, D.C.: ACE.

Bogue, D. O. 1959. *The Population of the United States.* Glencoe, Ill.: The Free Press.

California State Department of Education. 1960. *A Master Plan for Higher Education in California, 1960–1975.* Sacramento: CSDE.

Carlborg, F. W. 1968. *Introduction to Statistics.* Glenview, Ill. Scott Forsman.

Collins, C. C. 1969. *College Orientation: Education for Relevance.* Boston: Holbrook Press.

Collins, C. C. 1970. "Financing Higher Education: A Proposal." *Educational Record* Vol. 51:4 (Fall): 368–377. Washington, D.C.: American Council on Education.

Creager, J.; Astin, A.; Baruch, R.; and Bayer, A. 1968. *National Norms for Entering Freshmen—Fall 1968.* American Council on Education, Research Report 3(1). Washington, D.C.: American Council on Education.

Creager, J.; Astin, A.; Baruch, R.; and Bayer, A. 1969. *National Norms for Entering Freshmen—Fall 1968.* Washington, D.C.: American Council on Education.

Cross, K. Patricia. 1969. *The Junior Colleges' Role in Providing Postsecondary Education for All.* Berkeley, Calif.: Center for Research and Development in Higher Education.

Cross, K. Patricia. 1971. Access and Accommodation in Higher Education. In *The White House Conference on Youth,* pp. 67–82. Berkeley, Calif.: Center for Research and Development in Higher Education.

Darley, J. G. 1962. *Promise and Performance: A Study of Ability and Achievement in Higher Education.* Berkeley, Calif.: Center for the Study of Higher Education.

Educational Testing Service. 1964. *Cooperative Academic Ability Test Handbook.* Princeton, N. J.: Educational Testing Service.

Erik H. Erikson, "The Problem of Ego Identity" in Identity and the Life Cycle, *Psychological Issues,* 1959, Vol. 1, No. 1; and Erik H. Erikson, *Childhood and Society,* New York: Norton, 1950.

Flynt, Ralph C. M. "America's Resources of Undeveloped Talent." *School Life* 37:122–4, May 1955, Government Printing Office: Washington, D.C.

Froomkin, J. 1969. *Aspirations, Enrollments and Resources.* Washington, D.C.: U.S. Department of Health, Education, and Welfare.

Hansen, W. L., and Weisbrod, B. A. 1969. *Benefits, Costs and Finance of Public Higher Education.* Chicago: Markham.

Heist, P., and Webster, H. 1960a. Differential Characteristics of Student Bodies— Implications for Selection and Study of Undergraduates. In T. R. McConnell, ed., *Selection and Educational Differentiation,* pp. 91– 106. Berkeley, Calif.: University of California, Field Service Center; and Center for the Study of Higher Education.

Heist, P., and Webster, H. 1960b. A Research Orientation to Selection, Admission, and Differential Education. In H. T. Sprague, ed., *Research on College Students,* pp. 21–40. Boulder, Colo.: Western Inerstate Commission for Higher Education and the Center for the Study of Higher Education.

Heist, P., and Yonge, G. 1968. *Omnibus Personality Inventory: Form F, Manual.* New York: The Psychological Corporation.

Illinois Board of Higher Education. 1964. *A Master Plan for Higher Education in Illinois.* Springfield, Ill.: IBHE.

Kandel, D. B., and Lesser, G. S. 1969. "Parental and Peer Influences on Educational Plans of Adolescents." *American Sociological Review* 34: 213–223.

Keniston, K. 1966. *The Uncommitted: Alienated Youth in American Society.* New York: Harcourt, Brace, and World.

Knoell, Dorothy M., and Medsker, L. L. 1964. *Factors Affecting Performance of Transfer Students From Two- and Four-Year Colleges: With Implications for Coordination and Articulation,* U.S. Office of Education Cooperative Research Project No. 1133. Berkeley, Calif.: Center for the Study of Higher Education, University of California.

Marcia, J. E. 1966. "Development and Validation of Ego-Identity Status." *Journal of Personality and Social Psychology* 3:551–558.

Massachusetts Legislature. 1957. *Report of the Special Commission on Audit of State Needs.* Boston: Massachusetts Legislature.

Medsker, L. L., and Tillery, D. 1971. *Breaking the Access Barriers: A Profile of Two-Year Colleges,* Carnegie Commission on Higher Education. New York: McGraw-Hill.

Medsker, L. L., and Trent, J. 1965. *Factors Affecting College Attendance of High School Graduates From Varying Socioeconomic and Ability*

Levels, U.S. Office of Education Cooperative Research Project No. 438. Berkeley, Calif.: Center for Research and Development in Higher Education.

Rice, Mabel C., and Mason, P. L. 1965. *Residence and Migration of College Students.* Washington, D.C.: U.S. Department of Health, Education, and Welfare.

Sanford, N., ed. 1967. *The American College: A Psychological and Social Interpretation of the Higher Learning.* New York: Wiley Science Editions.

Simpson, R. L. "Parental Influence, Anticipatory Socialization, and Social Mobility." *American Sociological Review* 27: 517–522.

Spindt, H. A. 1959. Improving the Prediction of Academic Achievement. In *Selection and Educational Differentiation.* Berkeley, Calif.: University of California, Field Service Center; Center for Study of Higher Education. Pp. 15–29

"The Equality Fiction." *New Republic,* 1969, Vol. 161, pp. 23–24.

The Report of the Governor's Commission on Education Beyond the High School, North Carolina State Board of Education, 1962.

Tillery, D.; Donovan, D.; and Sherman, B. *SCOPE Questionnaire Grade Twelve.* Berkeley: Center for the Study of Higher Education, 1966c.

Tillery, D. 1969–70. "Will the Real Guidance Counselor Please Stand Up?" *College Board Review* (Winter):17–23.

Tillery, D.; Donovan, D.; and Sherman, Barbara. 1966a. *SCOPE Four-State Profiles, Grade Twelve, 1966.* New York: College Entrance Examination Board and The Center for Research and Development in Higher Education.

Tillery, D.; Donovan, D.; and Sherman, Barbara. 1966b. *SCOPE State Profile Grade Nine, 1966.* New York: College Entrance Examination Board and The Center for Research and Development in Higher Education.

Tillery, D.; Donovan, D.; and Sherman, Barbara. 1968. Helpfulness of Parents, School Personnel, and Peers to Students With Different Educational Aspirations. Paper read at the American Psychological Association Convention, San Francisco, August 30, 1968.

Trent, J. W., with Golds, Jenette. 1967. *Catholics in College: Religious Commitment and the Intellectual Life.* Chicago: Univ. of Chicago Press.

Trent, J. W., and Medsker, L. L. 1968. *Beyond High School: A Psycho-Sociological Study of 10,000 High School Graduates.* San Francisco; Jossey-Bass.

Trow, M. 1967. The Meaning of Impact. In *Proceedings of the 1966 Invitational Conference on Testing Problems,* pp. 25–33. Princeton, N. J.: Educational Testing Service.

Tussman, J. 1968. "The Collegiate Rite of Passage." *Experiment and Innovation: New Directions in Education at the University of California* 2:1–19.

U.S. Department of Commerce. 1960. *U.S. Census of Population: 1960, Vol. 1.* Washington, D.C.: U.S. Government Printing Office.

U.S. Department of Commerce. 1967. *Statistical Abstracts of the United States, 1967.* Washington, D.C.: U.S. Government Printing Office.

U.S. Department of Commerce. 1968. *Current Population Reports: Population*

Estimates, Series P-25, No. 384. Washington, D.C.: U.S. Government Printing Office.

U.S. Department of Commerce. 1970. *Statistical Abstracts of the United States, 1970.* Washington, D.C.: U.S. Government Printing Office.

U.S. Department of Commerce and U.S. Department of Labor. 1971. *The Social and Economic Status of Negroes in the United States, 1970.* Washington, D.C.: U.S. Government Printing Office.

U.S. Department of Health, Education, and Welfare. 1966–67. *Education Directory.* Washington, D.C.: U.S. Government Printing Office.

Wesman, A. G. 1953. Better Than Chance. In *Test Service Bulletin, No. 45,* p. 10. New York: The Psychological Corporation.

Willingham, W. W. 1969. *The Importance of Relevance in Expanding Post-Secondary Education.* New York: College Entrance Examination Board.

Willingham, W. W. 1970. *Free-Access Higher Education.* New York: College Entrance Examination Board.

Willingham, W., and Findikyan, N. 1969. *Patterns of Admission for Transfer Students.* New York: College Entrance Examination Board.

Index

About the Author

Dale Tillery received his Ph.D. in psychology and education from the University of California, Berkeley. He is currently professor of higher education at Berkeley and senior researcher at its Center for Research and Development in Higher Education. In recent years Professor Tillery has developed and directed experimental programs at the University of California for the preparation of college teachers and administrative leaders.

Professor Tillery has been a Fullbright Professor in Athens, Greece, and has performed educational development work in Africa and South America. His recent publications include two books for the Carnegie Commission Series on higher education: *The Open Door Colleges* (primary author) and *Breaking the Access Barriers* (co-author). He is also co-author of *Educational Goals, Attitudes and Behaviors: A Comparative Study of High School Seniors,* Ballinger Publishing Company, 1973. He served as a member of the United States team at the 1973 Paris Conference on the Future of Higher Education sponsored by the Organization for Economic Cooperation and Development.